Steve Parish
PUBLISHING

THE GREAT BARRIER REEF

A WORLD HERITAGE NATIONAL PARK

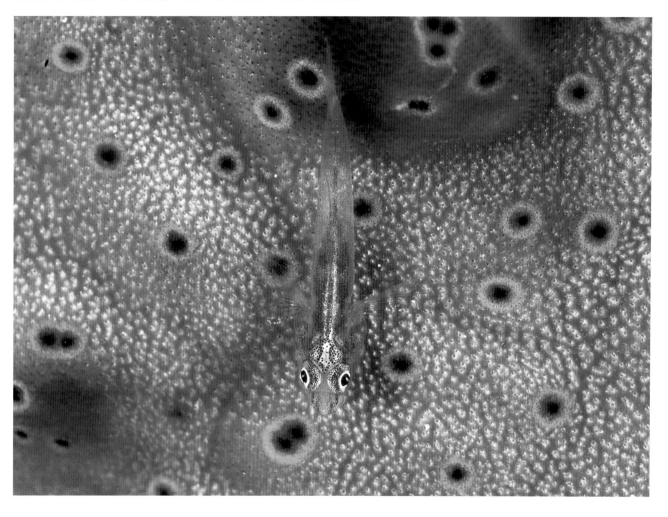

A small ghost goby *Pleurosicya* living
commensally on the mantle of a giant clam
Tridacna gigas.

PHOTOGRAPHY GARY BELL

TEXT DR TONY AYLING

FOREWORD

The creative eye of a marine photographer and the exacting mind of a scientist combine to create this exquisite book on the largest, most diverse and certainly most-threatened of all of the World Heritage Areas on Earth.

This spectacular book tells the story of the planet's largest World Heritage Area, told through the lens and words of two talented professionals. Gary Bell, the photographer, is one of few visual artists to have mastered the art of underwater photography in such a way that the two-dimensional images appear to draw you in and drag you under, immersing you in a miraculous submarine world. Accomplished in the use of artificial light in what is a largely blue-green world, Gary illuminates the reef's treasures and depicts each animal as an icon of the reef in its own right. From the gigantic whale to the diminutive shrimp, his lenses reveal vivid colour, texture and form that satisfies even the most ardent connoisseur of abstract art.

When one looks beyond the beauty of the animals and begins to ask questions about their lifestyles — the scientific observations of Dr Tony Ayling leap to the fore. Tony has been passionate about sea creatures since childhood, and over the past 25 years he has dived extensively and researched the Great Barrier Reef in its entirety. In doing so, he has developed the perceptive skills of an environmental interpreter and his text leads us on a journey through this remarkable ecosystem, using simple words that nevertheless enthrall and intrigue. As the publisher, and as an experienced diver and photographer myself, I wanted to craft a book that celebrates this spectacular World Heritage Area and awakens the artist, dreamer and naturalist within us all. Perhaps, by inspiring curiosity in a submerged world that few people see, we can likewise inspire the need to conserve this unique part of our planet.

This book's release is timely — it comes at a point in the Great Barrier Reef's long history where the human threat to its existence, by pollution, species degradation and climate change, has never been higher. It comes as a pertinent reminder that over 43% of the Earth's coral reefs are now degraded due to misuse and mismanagement. It comes as a warning that, sadly, another 40% are heading in that same direction. Most importantly it comes as a call to action in a world where as little as 1% of the Earth's valuable reef ecosystems are afforded any form of statutory protection.

So dive into this awe-inspiring world! See it, feel it, understand it through the eyes and mind of these two dedicated men, and join in the challenge to protect it — after all, if we do nothing, diving through the pages of a book may one day be the only way to appreciate this uniquely special underwater wonder.

Steve Parish — Publisher, Brisbane 2007

The richest coral communities are usually found on the exposed south-east-facing front reef, where the water is clear and currents sweep along the reef slope. Fast-growing Acropora *corals are common in this habitat — many of the corals shown here are only between 5–10 years old.*

Rich growth of *Acropora* corals on a reef slope.

CONTENTS

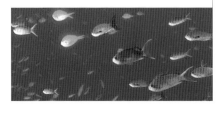

Each of the 2500 or so reefs that make up the Great Barrier Reef has been built up by stony corals over the past few hundred thousand years. As each coral colony grows and dies it contributes to the structure of the reefs as we see them today. Fishes and other animals consume coral and produce sand from their waste material.

Hook and Hardy reefs, offshore from the Whitsunday group of islands, with the blue line of the deep, current-swept channel separating them. A mosaic of patch reefs patterns the lagoon floor.

A school of fairy basslets aggregate together over coral. Schooling is a survival strategy employed by many fish species to avoid predation. Many eyes enhance the school's ability to detect predators, while weight of numbers affords individual fish better odds against being eaten. Schooling is also a statistically better way of finding a mate.

Fairy basslets *Pseudanthias dispar*.

INTRODUCTION

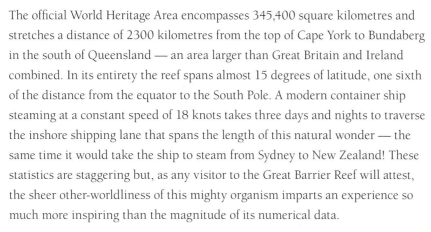

The Great Barrier Reef is an immense entity and a world-renowned phenomenon. Each year, over two million visitors from around the world spend time exploring this Australian icon, marvelling at the beauty and diversity of our planet's largest natural ecosystem.

The official World Heritage Area encompasses 345,400 square kilometres and stretches a distance of 2300 kilometres from the top of Cape York to Bundaberg in the south of Queensland — an area larger than Great Britain and Ireland combined. In its entirety the reef spans almost 15 degrees of latitude, one sixth of the distance from the equator to the South Pole. A modern container ship steaming at a constant speed of 18 knots takes three days and nights to traverse the inshore shipping lane that spans the length of this natural wonder — the same time it would take the ship to steam from Sydney to New Zealand! These statistics are staggering but, as any visitor to the Great Barrier Reef will attest, the sheer other-worldliness of this mighty organism imparts an experience so much more inspiring than the magnitude of its numerical data.

Despite being known as the world's largest coral reef, the Great Barrier Reef is not a single, continuous structure. It comprises about 1200 large offshore reefs (ranging from a kilometre to over 30 kilometres in length), as well as 1700 or so smaller patch reefs and inshore fringing reefs. Until relatively recently this vast mosaic remained mostly unknown and unexplored, save for the local knowledge garnered by a few hardy and intrepid fishermen. Although the inshore shipping channel has been thoroughly surveyed for many years, large areas of the Great Barrier Reef were not mapped or charted until late 1982 when the Great Barrier Reef Marine Park Authority released a set of maps generated from aerial photos and satellite imagery. Many individual reefs still remain unnamed, but every reef now has its own identifying number.

The human history of the Great Barrier Reef extends back 40,000 years to the first reef- and island-hopping Aborigines who entered the country via Torres Strait. With simple canoes and rafts they explored the many islands and cays of the Great Barrier Reef, feeding off its then untouched bounty and observing its strange evolution. During the last ice age (when sea levels were well over 100 metres lower than they are today) most of the reefs were exposed. Over many generations Aborigines witnessed the gradual retreat of the sea and watched as exposed reefs slowly became limestone islands and then, eventually, low hills on the coastal plain. In a very true sense the Aborigines used the entire reef area, living in caves along the edges of dried-out reef walls and hunting kangaroos where whales and dolphins now swim.

Although they relished the meat of turtles and dugong and gathered turtle eggs from seaside nests, the touch of Aborigines on the reef was light compared to the impact of European colonists. White entrepreneurs and settlers in small, well-built boats combed the dangerous waters of the reef, fishing and collecting all that could be sold or used. Coral for converting to lime; bêche-de-mer for drying and selling to the Chinese; oysters for their valuable shells and the bonanza of rare pearls; trochus shells for mother-of-pearl; and fish for drying and salting — all were gleaned from the reef in harvesting practices that resulted in much loss of life and vessel. Exploitation slowed once the numbers of valuable species dropped to uneconomic levels, but fishing and trawling operations with increasingly sophisticated vessels continued to harvest the entire reef until the creation of the marine park in the late 20th century.

In the early 1970s there was increasing concern that the Great Barrier Reef was being considered for oil exploration and drilling, was heavily overfished by an increasing fishing and trawling fleet, and was threatened by rapidly growing levels of coastal development and island and offshore tourism ventures. After commissioning a number of studies, the federal government reacted to public concern by passing a special act of parliament to establish the Great Barrier Reef Marine Park Authority (GBRMPA). This body was to oversee the creation and management of a marine park that encompassed the entire Great Barrier Reef and surrounding seas. The idea behind the marine park was not to completely protect the whole area, as is usually the case for terrestrial national parks, but to manage the region in a sustainable way that would allow existing user groups to continue reasonable activities within the marine park.

The first task of GBRMPA was to campaign for World Heritage listing for the Great Barrier Reef. UNESCO conferred this privileged status in October 1981. Over the next six years, the Great Barrier Reef was mapped in detail and divided into management sections that could be zoned to control their use. As zoning plans were progressively applied to each reef section, a few reefs became totally protected, "no-go" preservation zones and another 5% of reefs became "no-take" marine national park zones where fishing and collecting were forbidden. Trawling and commercial fishing were still permitted over much of the marine park, and tourist and recreational users could still visit most reefs. In July 2004 a revised zoning plan increased the no-take area within the Great Barrier Reef Marine Park — one-third of the total region is now off limits to fishermen and collectors. This sustainable zoning plan ensures the long-term preservation of the most significant reef habitats within the marine park.

GBRMPA and other government bodies have been encouraging research on the Great Barrier Reef for the past 30 years and scientists and other interested individuals have made important breakthroughs in understanding the complexity of the coral reef ecosystem. Coupled with this scientific study is media attention, which often focuses on the health of the reef and perceived threats to its viability. Consequently, we now have a better knowledge of the reef than we ever had in the past. Although we have come a long way in this process over the last three decades, it is both fascinating and humbling to realise that we have still barely scratched the surface of the vast mystery that is the Great Barrier Reef.

Fragile staghorn corals in shallow water are reduced to rubble by cyclonic waves. Storm waves can accumulate sand and rubble on the back edge of the reef flat, creating a low coral cay that may become vegetated by grass or specialist shrubs and trees such as the pisonia tree Pisonia grandis.

A cluster of Acropora staghorn corals on the shallow reef flat near Heron Island in the Capricorn–Bunker Group of reefs.

The stony skeletons of a diverse community of corals, growing on the dead remains of other corals, are the basic building blocks of the Great Barrier Reef. Sand and broken coral fragments fill the gaps between colonies and the whole mass is cemented by crustose coralline algae. Rich communities of fishes and other animals live with these corals — many of them survive by eating the plankton that provides about 30% of the corals' food needs.

Above: Various hard coral species, including several *Acropora* clumps, yellow-green *Porites* lichen and club-shaped *Acropora palifera* (right).

Opposite: Plankton-feeding fishes on a coral outcrop, including orange basslets *Anthias* cf. *cheirospilos* and blackaxil pullers *Chromis atripectoralis*.

Most stony corals are attached to the bottom and are made up of many separate small polyps — each with a mouth and a ring of stinging tentacles that trap plankton animals from the water. Mushroom corals are different, being each made up of a single large polyp that is free-living, lying unattached on the bottom as an adult.

Mouth of a mushroom coral *Fungia scutaria.*

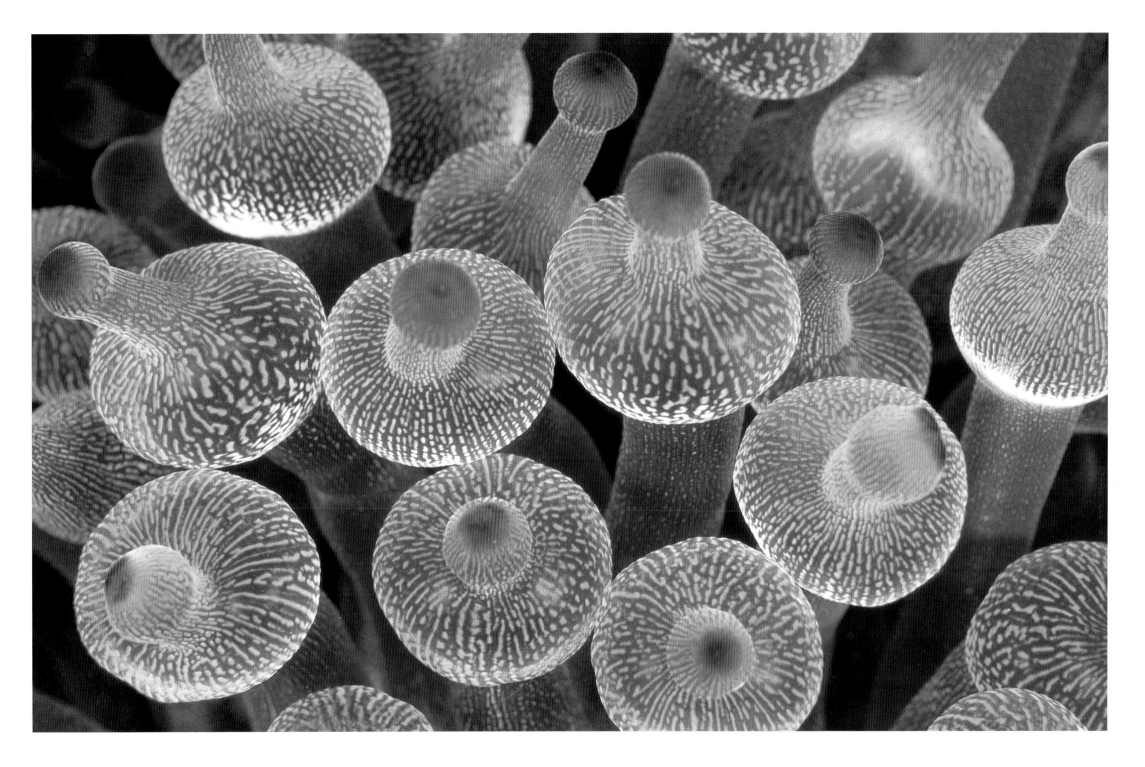

Stony corals are not the only reef animals to rely on symbiotic algae for a large portion of their food supply. Many sponges, soft corals, giant clams and foraminifera all have zooxanthellae in their tissues. The green-brown colour of these anemone tentacles comes from the chloroplasts of their algae.

Cluster of bulb-shaped tentacles from the sea anemone *Entacmea quadricolor*.

Reef animals lacking symbiotic algae rely on trapping plankton from the surrounding water to satisfy their nutritional needs. This "wall of mouths" quickly depletes the available food unless strong currents constantly bring in fresh supplies of plankton. These filter-feeding animals are often more brightly coloured than symbiotic corals.

Soft corals *Dendronephthya* with feather stars *Comantheria* sp. and green coral tree *Tubastra micracantha*.

Serpulid worms are also filter-feeders that live by trapping plankton from the surrounding water. Tiny, whip-like cilia line each pinule on the feeding crown and their constant beating drives water through this fine, filtering net. Other cilia, coated in mucus, trap food items and pass them down a groove in each filament to the mouth at the base of the crown.

Feather duster serpulid tube worm *Bispira* sp.

Not all planktonic animals are microscopic. Salps, comb jellies, siphonophores and sea jellies are all conspicuous, permanent members of the planktonic community. These blubber jellies do not have long stinging tentacles, but employ a network of tiny, plankton-feeding mouths on the club-like mouth-arms hanging beneath their bells.

A pair of blubber jellies *Catostylus mosaicus*.

Over 1500 different species of fishes live in the Great Barrier Reef World Heritage Area. Each of the varied groups of fishes has many representatives — for example, there are nine sweetlip species and eight anemonefish species in this region.

Above, left to right: A resting school of oblique-banded sweetlips *Plectorhinchus lineatus*; A blackback anemonefish *Amphiprion melanopus* nestled safely among its home tentacles.

Lurking, predatory fishes are often well comouflaged, resting unseen on the bottom while they wait for unwary prey to pass by. The branched protuberances on this scorpionfish help break up its body outline, allowing the fish to blend in with bottom growths. If a careless fish strays too close, the waiting predator explodes off the bottom and engulfs the prey within its huge upward-facing mouth.

Head of smallscale scorpionfish
Scorpaenopsis oxycephala.

Mandarinfish are members of the dragonet family Callionymidae *and are rarely seen by divers. They can "hover" by rapidly fanning their pectoral fins, using movements so swift that their fins appear blurred to the naked eye. These beautiful fish are usually less than 6 centimetres long and swim among live and dead coral close to the bottom, where they feed on small benthic invertebrates. The male is larger than the female and has a high dorsal fin flag, which he raises to impress the female during courtship displays.*

A courting pair of mandarinfish
Pterosynchiropus splendidus.

In a commensal relationship one party benefits while the other party receives no benefit but is not harmed. Shrimps living in anemones receive shelter and protection from predators, but the anemone derives no real benefit. Cleaner shrimps, particularly, feed on anemone mucus and also graze mucus and parasites from fishes that solicit the shrimps' attention.

Commensal cleaner shrimp *Pereclimenes holthuisi* on the anemone *Heteractis magnifica*.

Cleaner shrimps enjoy a true symbiotic relationship with their fish "clients". The cleaner shrimp gains protection from predation, coupled with access to an easy meal, while its clients receive peace of mind from the removal of parasites. However, it has been shown that these shrimps get most of their food from mucus nibbled off the fishes' skin — parasites make up only a small part of their intake.

A coral rockcod *Cephalopholis miniata* being attended to by a striped cleaner shrimp *Lysmata amboinensis*.

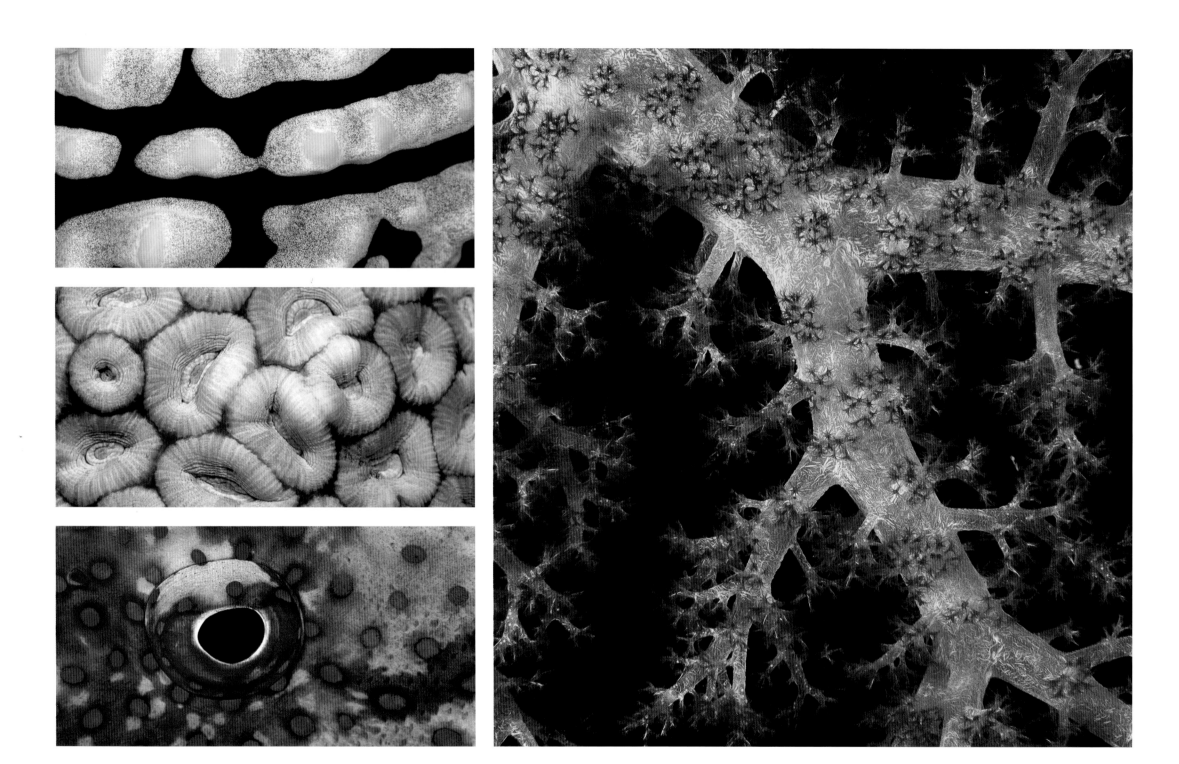

Bright colours and amazing patterns are everywhere on the Great Barrier Reef. Both colour and pattern serve a wide variety of biological purposes — as camouflage, as a visual distraction, as a toxicity warning, or as a necessary structural function (for example, the fan-shaped symmetry of lace corals is designed to increase the surface area of this organism's plankton-trapping "net").

Clockwise from top left: Close-up of the colour pattern of the nudibranch *Phyllidia varicosa*; *Dendronephthya* soft coral branches; The eye of the white-edge coronation trout *Variola albimarginata*; Polyps of the faviid hard coral *Favia rotundata* seen in close detail.

Manta rays are the largest of the rays and may reach lengths of more than 5 metres across their outspread wings. These graceful, gentle giants are also living plankton nets that swim, with their broad mouths agape, along current lines where plankton are concentrated. A fine net of gill rakers filter plankton and small fishes from the stream of water that pours out of open gill slits on the ray's underside.

A large manta ray *Manta birostris* swimming against a sunburst of light.

Another gentle ocean behemoth, the humpback whale, winters in warm reef waters. Here, mothers give birth, males sing to attract mates, and mating takes place. The whales do not feed during their winter sojourn, surviving on rich fat supplies stored during their summer feeding season in Antarctic waters. When Australian whaling ceased in 1962, fewer than 500 humpbacks remained in the east coast population. With total protection numbers have surged to 7000 and increase each year.

Humpback whale *Megaptera novaeangliae* with calf.

With silver-white tips and trailing edges on all their fins, silvertips are one of the reef's most attractive sharks. They patrol the front of outer reefs throughout the Great Barrier Reef World Heritage Area, usually in water over 30 metres deep. Silvertips are large sharks that grow to about 3 metres in length and may behave aggressively towards divers; however, they have never been implicated in attacks on humans.

Silvertip shark *Carcharhinus albimarginatus*.

Tourism is a key industry of the Great Barrier Reef World Heritage Area and each year more than two million visitors enjoy the delights of its warm waters and mesmerising coral reef communities.

A snorkeller examines plate corals
Acropora hyacinthus.

HISTORY & EVOLUTION OF CORAL REEFS

Limestone reefs, formed by corals and other invertebrates with hard skeletons, have been growing in shallow, tropical waters for hundreds of millions of years.

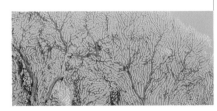

From 480–350 million years ago there was an extended period when reefs thrived throughout the world's tropical oceans. These reefs were made up of tabulate and rugose corals, which were unrelated to modern scleractinian corals, along with stromatoporoid sponges and calcareous algae. None of these reef builders survived the mass extinction at the end of the Permian period 250 million years ago, but the remains of these ancient reefs are scattered throughout Australia — eroded limestone hills containing fossils of the myriad organisms that lived among them. A fossilised barrier reef, much like the modern Great Barrier Reef, is now a meandering limestone range running along the northern edge of the Canning Basin in Western Australia. This reef may have been about 1000 kilometres long and is estimated to be over 350 million years old.

Coral reefs can only thrive in the tropics where warmer water temperatures promote the chemical processes that allow calcium to be deposited from seawater. Coral reef ecosystems cannot exist in water where the winter water temperature drops much below 18°C. Although individual corals can live in southern Australia, where temperatures drop below 12°C, they do not form reefs in these cold waters. The digestive processes of many groups of coral reef fishes are also temperature-dependant and these fishes cannot survive in cooler waters. Modern reef animals have been around since the early Tertiary period, shortly after the demise of the dinosaurs, and are less than 50 million years old. Most of the species of corals and fishes that are common on reefs today evolved at the start of the Miocene epoch, about 24 million years ago, and have remained remarkably similar ever since.

Coral reefs could not grow in Australia 50 million years ago. At that time the Australian continent was newly separated from Antarctica and lay between 40 and 60 degrees south, well into the cold temperate region. Over the following tens of millions of years Australia drifted rapidly north at the incredible rate of 6 centimetres a year, moving six metres closer to the tropics with each passing century. About 15 million years ago Australia finally entered the tropics and collided with the Asian plate. It is possible that some coral reefs began to form in the far north at this time, but major reef growth did not begin on the north-east coast until about 2 million years ago, when coral reefs began to form on the Coral Sea Rise. There is a lot of debate about the age of the Great Barrier Reef but, as far as it is possible to tell, coral reefs have only been present in the Great Barrier Reef region for the past 500,000 years or so. While we know that reefs (in some form) have been present for 500,000 years, their evolution has remained in a constant state of flux over this time.

For the past 4 million years or more the Earth has undergone cycles of alternating glaciation and warming, with corresponding falls and rises in sea level. As temperatures fall and glaciers build up during ice ages, millions of cubic kilometres of water are locked up and sea levels drop. During ice ages, sea levels may be well over 100 metres lower than they are during the warmer interglacial period, when many glaciers melt. Geologists have estimated that there have been about ten glacial cycles over the past 200,000 years, each with associated sea level changes. The developing coral reefs in the Great Barrier Reef region would have had a stop-start history. During glacial periods the reefs would have dried out and become limestone hills. Corals and fishes would have recolonised these eroded hills as sea levels rose again during the next interglacial period and reef ecosystems were re-established.

It has been estimated that active reef growth on the Great Barrier Reef has only been possible for about a quarter of the past 200,000 years. At the height of each glacial period, when sea levels were at their lowest, reefs would have been confined to a narrow fringe along the edge of the continental shelf. Australia's climate was wetter at that time and run-off from rivers directly onto the remaining fringing reefs would have limited the area that could support these enduring reef communities. Siltation and freshwater run-off from large river systems would have made large areas of the coast unsuitable for coral reefs. The predominant south-east trade winds would have blown directly onto the coast, keeping sediments suspended and making conditions less than ideal for reef survival and growth. As sea levels rose again during each interglacial period, larvae from corals and other animals on these fringing reef patches would have reclaimed their former territories and continued reef growth.

The last ice age began about 23,000 years ago. At its peak, about 17,000 years ago, the sea level was 120–150 metres lower than it is today. Then, as at many times before, the reefs as we know them were just limestone hills on the vegetated coastal plain. The rise in sea levels over the following 10,000 years, as the massive glaciers that covered much of the cold temperate regions of the world began to melt, was very rapid. Average rises of about a centimetre a year have been estimated for this period, although some studies suggest that the rate fluctuated and, during times of rapid change, sea levels may have rushed up at many times that speed. Modern sea levels were only reached about 6000 years ago and have been unusually stable since that time, allowing the reefs of the Great Barrier Reef to develop to the lush condition that we see today. This turbulent history suggests that these coral reefs are not the stable, fragile ecosystems they are often portrayed to be.

ACROSS THE SHELF

No two of the many thousands of reefs that make up the Great Barrier Reef are the same. During its recent rezoning exercise, the Great Barrier Reef Marine Park Authority identified 30 major groups of different reef types that made up the Great Barrier Reef and required protection.

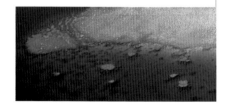

Although reefs within these groups have many similarities, none are identical. Many factors influence the structure of a particular reef, and therefore what animals will live and breed around that reef. The major shaping force, however, is the position of a reef across the continental shelf. Since the modern era of reef research began 25 years ago, scientists have realised that the corals, fishes and other reef animals that make up a reef were very different on fringing reefs on the inner-shelf from those on barrier reefs near the outer edge of the shelf.

INNER-SHELF REEFS

On the mainland coast there is a thick wedge of fine sediment that has been washed out of rivers over the past 6000 years and deposited in shallow water on the inner-shelf. These rivers also flush nutrients off the land and into the coastal waters. The prevailing south-east trade winds keep these sediments and nutrients suspended in water close to the coast, creating turbid conditions around inshore reefs. Underwater visibility on these inner-shelf reefs is often less than a metre and only exceeds 5 metres during the extended calm spells of weather that sometimes occur during the summer months. These conditions are not pleasant for divers exploring coastal reefs; most fish species do not like them either, hence only a few fish species are common on these dirty inshore reefs.

Surprisingly, corals often thrive on these inner-shelf reefs, creating extensive lush gardens that are usually dark brown, rather than the vibrant colours people associate with coral reefs. Coral reefs usually exist in waters that are nutrient deserts, but the relatively rich nutrients flushed off the land into inner-shelf waters provide plenty of food for seaweeds or algae. Long brown fronds of bladder weed or *Sargassum* often form dense forests in a narrow band around the inner edge of many coastal coral reefs; only a few corals can grow under this algal forest. Large algal plants such as this are not found on offshore reefs in the Great Barrier Reef region. These inshore fringing reefs are very shallow and are usually no more than 10 metres deep on the outer edge, where the coral meets the sand. They are also very young and have developed only over the past 6000 years, once sea level reached its current height.

There are many high islands near the coast throughout the Great Barrier Reef and most are surrounded by fringing reefs similar to those on the mainland coast. The water is usually not quite as turbid around these island fringing reefs and underwater visibility can exceed 10 metres in good conditions. Across the middle of the continental shelf there is usually a gap between islands and offshore reefs — through this gap the large shipping channel snakes its way up the Queensland coast.

MID-SHELF REEFS

Most individual reefs that make up the Great Barrier Reef are mid-shelf reefs. The majority are 5–30 kilometres long and are scattered across the shelf in water 30–60 metres deep. There is very little terrestrial influence on these reefs and the nutrient and sediment load in the water is much lower than on the coast. Visibility on these reefs ranges from 10–25 metres and the corals are more colourful than those on inner-shelf reefs. Diversity of plants and animals is higher on mid-shelf reefs than on coastal reefs, and these reefs offer more interesting diving than island and mainland fringing reefs.

OUTER-SHELF REEFS

The other major group of reefs is those that are positioned near the outer edge of the continental shelf, where they are bathed in the clear waters of the open Coral Sea. These outer-shelf reefs are among the most spectacular in the region, with steep drop-offs, a very diverse community, and deep blue, crystal-clear water. Underwater visibility ranges from 20–50 metres on these reefs, giving divers panoramic views of their steep walls, caves and coral bommies.

On the northern third of the Great Barrier Reef the outer-shelf reefs form an almost continuous narrow line of reefs known as the outer barrier rampart. These reefs are right on the edge of the continental shelf and their front face falls rapidly from the reef crest, where the ocean swells break endlessly, vertically down to depths of 30–60 metres or more. From the base of these underwater cliffs the bottom slopes off steeply into the ocean depths. Large pelagic fish such as tuna and marlin patrol these ramparts, and huge schools of trevallies check out the feeding opportunities. To the south of this outer barrier line, the outer-shelf reefs become more scattered. Towards the south end of the Great Barrier Reef, these reefs are small and widely spaced. Divers in the know seek out diving opportunities on these wonderful outer-shelf reefs.

Even more spectacular are the oceanic detached reefs that rise up from deep water beyond the outer barrier reefs. Surrounded by steep drop-offs, they are usually bathed in turquoise water that is devoid of nutrients and mostly free of the planktonic life which reduces water clarity. Detached reefs, such as Raine Island and Great Detached Reef near the northern tip of the Great Barrier Reef, are rarely visited by divers but provide unique conditions that set them apart from the rest of the reef. Sheer walls, clear water, lots of sharks and turtles, and diverse and unusual fish species make these reefs the pinnacle of underwater experiences on the Great Barrier Reef.

Opposite: Heron Island, a coral cay in the Capricorn–Bunker group of reefs.

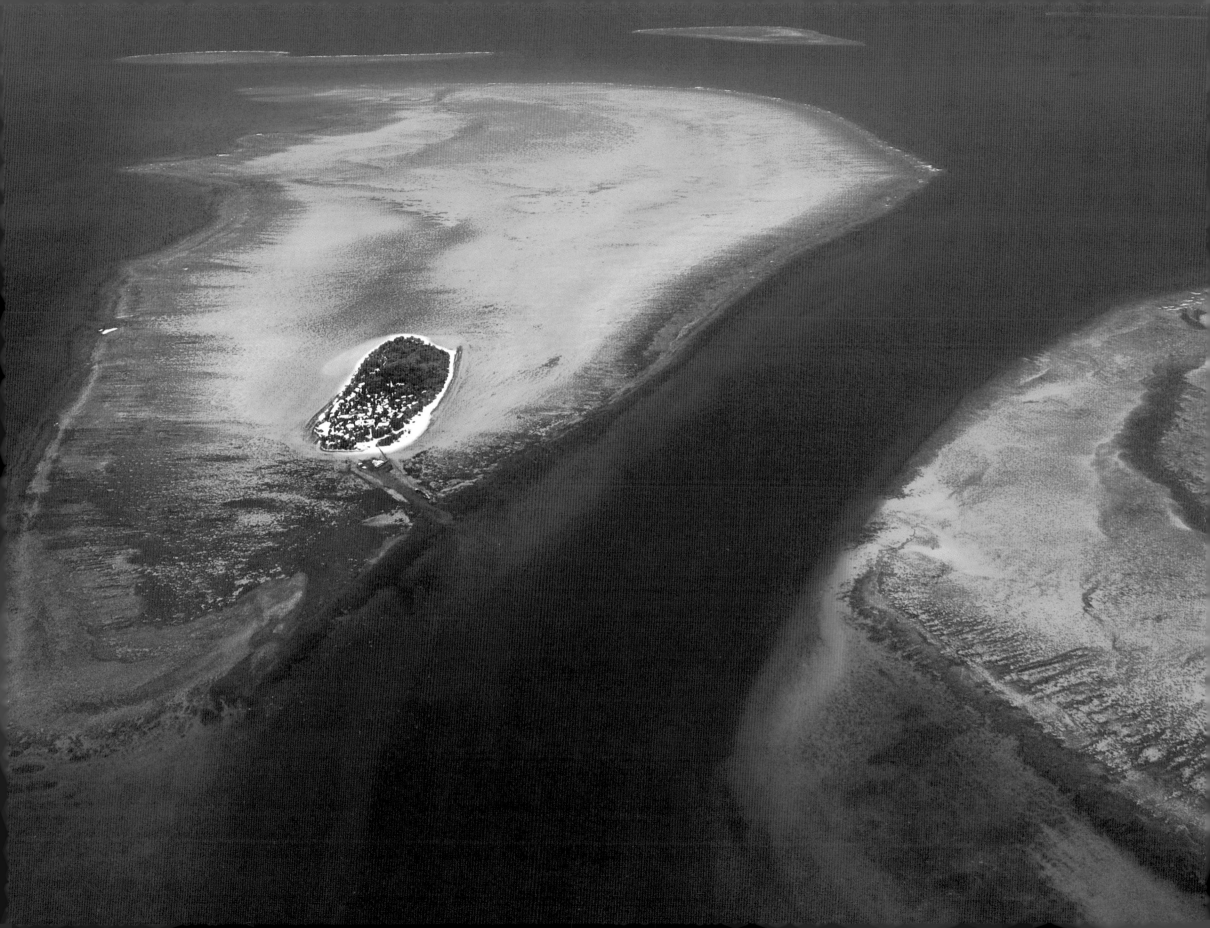

A rich fringing reef surrounds Lizard Island — a granite island 30 kilometres offshore to the north of Cooktown. In 1770, Captain James Cook climbed Lizard Island's 400-metre peak to help negotiate a safe passage through the maze of reefs that confronted him. Today, a resort and a research station help tourists and scientists alike get a glimpse of this beautiful island.

Lizard Island, a high continental island on the northern Great Barrier Reef.

The northern outer barrier reefs lie along the outer edge of the continental shelf. The white line of ocean waves breaking on the outside of these reefs marks the point where they slope steeply into the cobalt depths. A number of coral patch reefs (or bommies) can be seen on the protected sides of these reefs.

Looking north along the line of outer barrier reefs from No-Name (foreground) to Yonge, Carter and Day Reefs.

THE REEF ENVIRONMENT

It would be wonderful if the waters of the Great Barrier Reef were always as tranquil, calm and blue as they are constantly depicted in tourist brochures and photographs. The reality, however, is quite different.

WINDS

The Great Barrier Reef lies in the south-east trade wind belt for much of the year, so the waters are often rough. Huge high-pressure systems over southern Australia drive these winds onto the tropical coast, with successive highs causing a week-long burst of strong winds followed by a lull of a few days before a new high-pressure ridge is established. Winds are often 20–30 knots during these trade wind bursts and in a bad year the lulls between highs may be rare or non-existent. The trade wind season usually stretches from late March through to October. During the monsoon season from November to March the wind pattern on the Great Barrier Reef is variable. Bursts of strong south-east winds still occur through this period but the lulls between highs become longer and may stretch out to several weeks. It is during these beautiful calm spells that photographers take to the air and sea and present us with all those "typical" barrier reef images.

The north-west monsoon may push south over the Great Barrier Reef region during the November to March period, bringing hot north-westerly winds, thunderstorms and squalls. This time of the year is also the cyclone season. Cyclones are concentrated balls of low pressure with winds between 100 and 300 kilometres per hour, depending on the cyclone intensity. Every year an average of five or six cyclones form in the northern Coral Sea, but many of these track off into the Pacific and only two or three usually move into the Great Barrier Reef region and cross the Queensland coast.

Cyclonic winds usually only affect an area about 50 kilometres across, but within this zone the destruction they cause to the reef is unbelievable. Seas whipped up by cyclonic winds are phenomenal and swells in the open ocean outside the reef can peak at more than 12 metres. Even in the shelter of the reef seas can reach 5–10 metres and the power of these waves can devastate coral communities. Fragile branching coral colonies and delicate whorls and vases are reduced to rubble banks. Large corals may be broken apart or overturned. Drifts of broken corals are swept to and fro by the tremendous power of the waves, grinding and abrading corals that are strong enough to withstand the force of the smashing water. Exposed parts of reefs impacted by a severe cyclone are almost completely stripped of living coral, leaving a few battered colonies scattered here and there in a moonscape of destruction. This damage is not limited to shallow water where the waves normally break, it may extend down to depths of more than 30 metres. Many other reef animals are destroyed along with the corals and a lot of the reef-associated fishes perish.

On average, every part of the Great Barrier Reef is hit by a cyclone once every 20 years or so, experiencing a severe impact about every 100 years.

Large coral masses probably survive these destructive episodes, but the rest of the coral community must rebuild itself from scratch. The reef has developed in this area and reached its present condition in spite of this sporadic devastation.

WATER TEMPERATURE

Warm sea temperatures also power cyclones — paradoxically, the same warm water that enables coral reef formation, can also lead to its destruction. Water temperatures on the Great Barrier Reef do not vary as greatly as they do in more temperate waters. On offshore reefs the annual temperature range is only 6 °C, with temperatures reaching a low of 24 °C on the northern reef and 22 °C at the southern extremity of the main offshore body of the reef. Corresponding maximum temperatures are 30 °C in the north and 28 °C in the south. Although the offshore reefs of the Great Barrier Reef span a latitudinal range from 10–23 degrees south, the temperature difference between these two extremes is only 2 °C at any one time. On inshore reefs, where the water is shallower and more rapidly affected by air temperature, the fluctuations in temperature may be more extreme. The Great Barrier Reef is the place to go if you want to swim in warm water — temperatures on these fringing reefs reach a winter low of a tepid 19 °C and a summer high of 31 °C. Temperatures are even warmer during El Niño events and colder during La Niña periods.

There is concern that global warming will make the Great Barrier Reef waters even warmer. When water temperatures exceed 31 °C for more than a few weeks, tiny symbiotic algae associated with reef-building corals start to generate toxins and are expelled by corals, leading to so-called coral bleaching. Unless the temperature falls again, the corals soon die without the algae. Understandably, some sections of the scientific community worry that global warming will spell the demise of many Great Barrier Reef corals.

TIDES

As well as winds and temperature, the physical environment of the reef is controlled by water movements. Ocean currents are generally weak within the Great Barrier Reef region and tidal currents are also slight. However, the huge shallow bay of Broad Sound just north of the town of Rockhampton generates a tidal peak of around 10 metres rise and fall. Although tides are much lower on the outer reefs, the tidal currents on the 300-kilometre-long section of reefs offshore from the Broad Sound area can race around the reefs at speeds of 3–9 knots during spring tides, making diving very exciting but also dangerous. These rushing waters also push plenty of planktonic food onto the reefs, creating rich areas with abundant fish and coral species.

The dark blue channels that separate these reefs are 60-metre-deep, steep-sided gutters that funnel the strong tidal currents running through this part of the Great Barrier Reef. A tourist destination pontoon can be seen against the side of Hardy Reef in the centre right of the picture.

Above: Hook, Line, Sinker and Hardy Reefs offshore from the Whitsunday Islands.

The south-east trade winds blow onto the Great Barrier Reef region for at least eight months of the year. Consequently, the front, south-east-facing sides of reefs are often pounded by large waves. During storms and cyclones the wave turbulence breaks up corals on the exposed reef fronts. Outer reefs often have very little coral on the reef crest where these waves break.

Above: Breaking waves along the front of the outer barrier reef.

Opposite: Breaking waves form underwater storm clouds over a diver on the reef crest.

DIVERSITY

The Great Barrier Reef is an incredibly diverse marine ecosystem. The number of different animal and plant species that live together to form the Great Barrier Reef is truly astounding and, for a first time visitor, wondrously beguiling.

The Great Barrier Reef's level of biodiversity is unmatched anywhere else on the planet. Everywhere on the reef, different species thrive and each habitat introduces a surreal roll call of intriguing life forms. Over 20,000 animal and plant species are thought to inhabit the Great Barrier Reef World Heritage Area, but many of these groups have been very poorly studied and the actual number may be much greater. While this number may seem high, it does not include the many thousands of microscopic planktonic and bottom-dwelling animals, plants and bacteria.

The reef is home to over 400 species of algae or seaweeds; 37 different mangroves; 15 sea grasses; more than 1500 sponges; 360 stony corals; around 500 other cnidarians (including soft corals, black corals, sea jellies and hydroids); more than 2000 flatworms; at least 500 polychaete worms; hundreds of worm species in other groups; between 5000–8000 molluscs or sea shells; about 7500 crustaceans (a figure that includes over 1000 crab and shrimp species); around 400 bryozoans; 630 different echinoderm species; 330 ascidians or sea squirts; 125 sharks and rays; more than 1500 species of bony fish; 6 turtle species; 17 sea snakes; 200 birds; 23 cetaceans; the dugong and the estuarine crocodile. There is something in this list to keep everyone interested and enough identification problems to keep an army of scientists busy for the next century. It is unlikely that we will ever have a comprehensive list of all the plants and animals that dwell on the Great Barrier Reef.

Although we know a lot about terrestrial animals and plants there are still huge gaps in our knowledge of marine groups. New fish species are regularly discovered on the Great Barrier Reef. Groups such as soft corals and sponges contain many species that have either never been described or have dry museum descriptions and illustrations that have never been linked to live counterparts on the reef. It might be possible to recognise all the sea grasses in the Great Barrier Reef region (there are only about 15 species), but even for a simple, small group like this there are a number of identification problems and potentially undescribed species that still need to be classified. Whales and dolphins have been studied for hundreds of years and no new species had been described for over 50 years until Australian researchers revealed they had found a new species in 2005. What had commonly been known as the Irrawaddy dolphin was in fact an undescribed species now named the Australian snubfin dolphin *Orcaella heinsohni*. Researchers also think that the dwarf minke whale, well known on the northern Great Barrier Reef, is another previously undescribed cetacean.

So, why are there so many different plants and animals on the Great Barrier Reef? Such high biodiversity has probably come about as a result of the long history of modern reefs and the large geographic range of the coral reef

ecosystem. Reefs have been around for about 25 million years in their present form and, since the process of speciation takes about 10,000 years, enough time has passed for a large number of species to evolve. Given that thousands of similar reefs are found throughout the Indian and Pacific Oceans, there are many opportunities for new species to evolve in isolation from their parent populations. These species increase the reef's overall diversity whenever they re-invade the region they originated from — becoming bona fide new species that are unable to breed with their parent species. Different coral reef animal groups have repeated this process many thousands of times over the past 25 million years, enabling reefs at the centre of the Indo-Pacific to experience an extremely high diversity of plant and animal species.

One important consequence of the high species diversity on the Great Barrier Reef is that it makes for a very resilient community. In many simple, low-diversity, temperate water communities the inter-relationships of the different animals and plants form a simple chain. There may only be a single large predator, one or two scavengers and minimal herbivores. In such a community the removal or reduction in numbers of a single species may have far-reaching consequences and throw the whole system into disarray. Conversely, in a high-diversity system like the Great Barrier Reef, there are hundreds of species that could occupy any link in the chain that binds the members of the community. Instead of a simple chain, this system is a complicated network with room for redundancy. Totally removing a single species may impact upon one or two specialist species that depend on it, but the network quickly rearranges itself and the stability of the reef as a whole remains intact. In all probability, removing half the total species from the Great Barrier Reef would result in a short period of readjustment before the remaining species continued life as a fully functioning community.

This process can be seen in action when we travel to the low-diversity reefs at the fringe of the Indo-Pacific region. Reefs in places like Hawaii and Easter Island may have only one-tenth of the diversity of the Great Barrier Reef, but these dramatically fewer species still combine to form healthy, functioning reefs. A similar process exists within the Great Barrier Reef. No two reefs have the same mix of species and abundance, but all form a vigorous, working reef community. Because of this complexity and redundancy, coral reefs are unusually resilient ecosystems — a far cry from the fragile, delicately balanced communities they are often painted to be.

Opposite: The Great Barrier Reef's incredible biodiversity is evident in this photograph where approximately ten coral species and ten fish species are visible.

Over 360 stony coral species are found on the Great Barrier Reef — almost half the worldwide total of 794 species. Stony corals cover a huge range of growth forms, colours and sizes. They may be single polyps smaller than 20 centimetres in diameter, massive boulder corals over 10 metres across or a staghorn thicket 100 metres across.

Boulder coral *Porites* sp. and yellow *Porites lichen* coral.

Clockwise from left: *Acropora tenuis*, a clump-forming branching coral; Mouth detail of a solitary mushroom coral *Fungia* sp.; *Pocillopora verrucosa*; *Symphyllia recta*.

Clockwise from top left: Blue ascidian *Rhopalaea* sp., Green ascidian *Didemnum* sp. and soft coral *Clavularia* sp.; A simple ascidian or sea squirt *Polycarpa aurata*; The mouth detail of a large anemone *Heteractis magnifica*; Fire hydroid *Macrorhynchia philippina*.

Apart from stony corals, thousands of species of other attached invertebrates reside on the Great Barrier Reef, including sponges, hydroids, sea anemones, soft corals, gorgonians, black corals and ascidians.

Large gorgonian fan *Melithaea* sp.

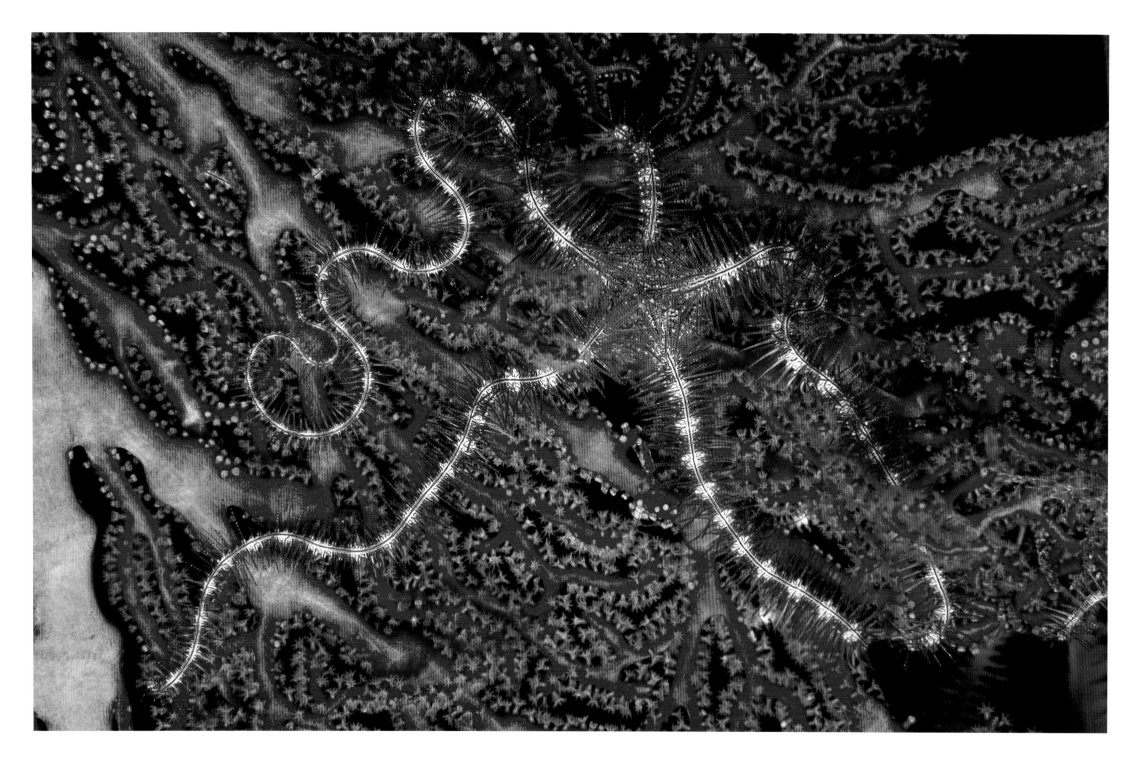

More than 15,000 different mobile invertebrates walk, crawl, slide, glide or swim among the bottom growth of Great Barrier Reef coral reefs. These animals include myriad worms, crabs, shrimps and other crustaceans, a multitude of different molluscs and a huge variety of echinoderms, such as sea stars, brittle stars, feather stars, sea urchins and holothurians.

Spiny brittle star *Ophiothrix* sp. on gorgonian fan *Melithaea* sp.

Clockwise from top left: A hairy hermit crab *Dardanus lagopodes*; Colourful flatworm *Pseudoceros gravieri*; An allied cowrie *Diminovula alabaster* feeding on the soft coral *Dendronephthya*; A bright red sea star *Fromia indica*.

More than 1500 species of bony fishes live in Great Barrier Reef waters and all are resplendent in their various shapes, sizes and patterns. For each closely related group of fishes there are many variations of a common theme, with each species often having several distinct colour patterns.

Clockwise from top left: Spotfin lionfish *Pterois antennata*; Newly settled larva of common lionfish *Pterois volitans*; Young of the common lionfish *Pterois volitans*; Common lionfish *Pterois volitans*.

Opposite: Zebra lionfish *Dendrochirus zebra*.

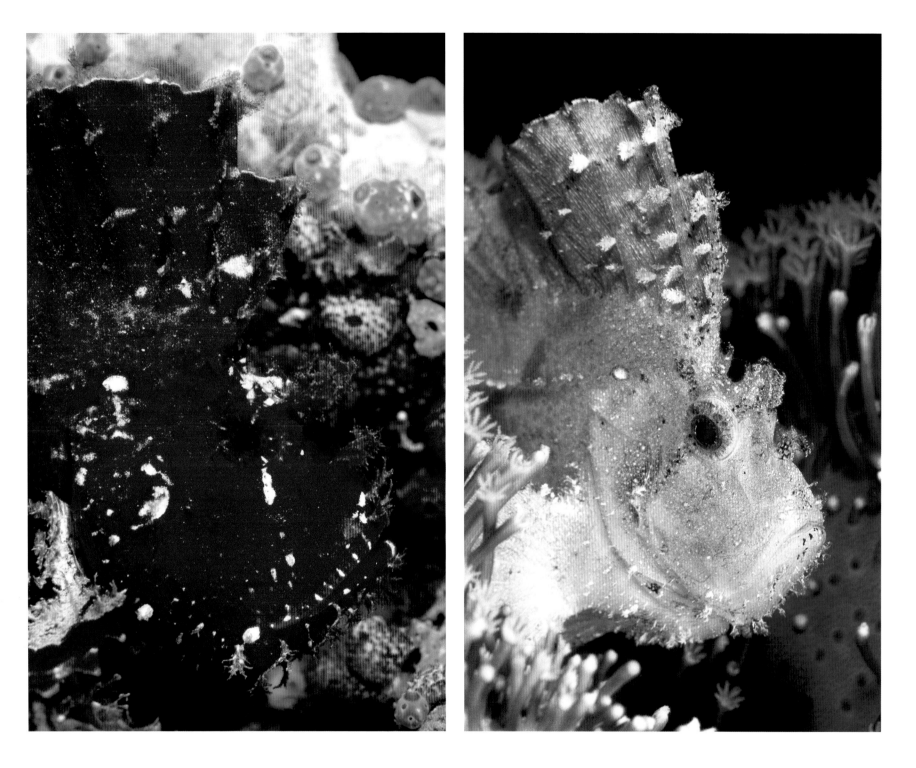

Some fish species are polymorphic, which means they have several different colour patterns. These colour patterns are fixed and an individual does not change from one form to another during its life. Scientists do not understand why certain fishes are polymorphic. The leaf scorpionfish shown here may be either bright red or pale yellow in colour.

Above, left to right: Head detail of the leaf scorpionfish *Taenianotus triacanthus*; Yellow colour form of the leaf scorpionfish.

Collectively, reef fish exhibit an incredible range of colours and shapes. Many use bright colours as either an overt warning to predators, or as a disruptive pattern to confuse predators. Colours are also used as signals to relay how a particular fish is feeling, or as spectacular displays to attract mates. Colour patterns, and changes in these patterns, form a language that many fishes use to communicate with each other.

Clockwise from top left: Harlequin filefish *Oxymonacanthus longirostris*; Eastern clown anemonefish *Amphiprion percula*; Clown triggerfish *Balistoides conspicillum*; Purple firegoby *Nemateleotris decora*.

THE REEF BUILDERS

Without stony corals (and the magic of their symbiotic relationship with tiny single-celled algae called "zooxanthellae") there would be no Great Barrier Reef.

Modern coral reefs are built upon the accumulated skeletons of thousands of years of stony coral growth. The coral skeletons are mixed with "spicules" (which form the skeletal structure of soft corals and sponges) and cemented together by the prolific growth of pink coralline algae. Cyclones smash up coral colonies and redistribute them as rubble, more corals grow on top of the dead and damaged colonies, more algal cementing consolidates the whole mass and in a slow, rather erratic, process a vast reef is created.

Compared with temperate oceans, tropical seas have relatively low nutrient levels and cannot support rich plankton communities. This lack of plankton makes many tropical seas so clear and perfect for diving. Most benthic encrusting animals (those attached to the bottom) get their food by filtering plankton from the surrounding water, but if plankton levels are low this lifestyle does not provide enough energy to live and grow rapidly. Many reef organisms overcome this problem by forming symbiotic relationships with algae.

In a symbiotic relationship both members of the partnership benefit from living together. In the case of the stony coral–zooxanthellae marriage, the algae receives three benefits. The first benefit is security: the algae is nestled safe within the living cells of corals. The second benefit is carbon dioxide (the raw material necessary for photosynthesis), received as a by-product from the coral's respiration. The third benefit is the steady supply of chemical nutrients from the corals' excretion. In return, the corals receive a supply of fixed carbon food from the algae and can use the oxygen that algae produce as a by-product of photosynthesis. This cosy relationship gives stony corals almost three-quarters of the food they need to survive, grow and reproduce.

As a result of this reliance on algae, corals behave a lot like plants. They need exposure to sunlight and have adopted flattened or spreading growth forms to maximise light absorption. Corals cannot live under shaded overhangs or in caves; they thrive only in shallow water. Light is absorbed rapidly in water — at depths of more than 60 metres there is not enough light for most corals to survive. Corals that do survive in the dim blue light below 50 metres form thin, wide plates in order to harness all the light they can for their algae. The richest, most luxuriant corals grow in water less than 20 metres deep, where there is plenty of sunlight for the symbiotic algae they rely on.

Zooxanthellae give corals most of their colour. Coral tissues are clear and colourless, allowing maximum light to penetrate their tissues and feed their zooxanthellae. Dark pigments absorb light more readily than pale colours, and in turbid coastal waters zooxanthellae adopt a dark brown colouration to absorb as much light as they can. Corals cannot grow at depths below 12 metres on dirty fringing reefs because light levels are too low. A coral without zooxanthellae turns stark white; hence the term "bleaching" to describe corals that have ejected their algae. Symbiotic algae provide corals with a lot more than colour — without zooxanthellae, corals could not survive and grow in the nutrient deserts that are tropical seas.

Stony corals employ different growth strategies. Some grow rapidly and cover space quickly, laying down a thin, fragile skeleton. These corals often have a branching form, rising up above other corals towards the light. Fast-growing staghorn and clumping *Acropora* corals, or whorl-forming *Montipora* corals, are the weeds of the coral world, spreading rapidly over damaged areas and dominating all the space they can. All their energy is expended on growth. These corals do not bother laying down a solid skeleton or developing sophisticated forms of defence (such as the production of toxic chemicals). These weedy corals can increase in size by more than 30 centimetres per year but they are easily broken during strong swells and storms. They are also the preferred food of most coral-eating animals. At the other end of the spectrum are the slow-growing, massive corals such as *Porites* boulder corals and *faviid* brain corals. These corals lay down dense, spherical skeletons but only increase in size by about a centimetre a year. Many of these corals produce chemicals that make them unpalatable, and they are more resistant to storms.

Corals do not die of old age. Unless they are broken up by cyclonic waves or eaten by other animals they live and grow for thousands of years. Large parts of a colony may be eaten or shattered, but the sections that remain continue growing. Single colonies may split into separate colonies — spreading out over a large area but retaining the same genotype and fusing together whenever these separate colonies next meet. Some spreading coral colonies may span 100 metres across. Massive corals lay down annual growth rings in their skeletons in the same way that trees do in their trunks. Scientists have found that large boulder corals over 10 metres in diameter may be more than 1000 years of age.

Reef corals' lack of mobility presents a major dilemma when other corals or encrusting animals shade or grow over them. Competition for space among different colonies unfolds in slow motion, compared to the territorial jockeying of mobile animals, but it is no less fierce. Some corals try to loom over intruding neighbours; others employ stinging tentacles to kill competitors, and some secrete toxins that force neighbours to keep their distance. Slow-growing but solid boulder corals simply endure, waiting for future cyclones to raze the fast-growing corals that attempt to engulf them.

Opposite: Massive coral colony *Favia stelligera.*

Coral species grow at markedly different rates. All the Acropora corals are fast-growing and can increase in diameter by 20–40 centimetres a year. The branches on staghorn Acropora colonies can increase in length by up to 15 centimetres in a year. At the other extreme, slow-growing rounded faviid corals only increase in diameter by about a centimetre a year.

A group of fast-growing Acropora corals.

Most stony corals are not brightly coloured because their colours come from the photosynthetic pigments of their symbiotic zooxanthellae. Brown-tinged yellow, green or blue are the usual colours, although some species display brighter pigments in their coral skeletons — usually in the branch tips.

Purple-tipped *Acropora* clumps surrounded by yellow-green branches of fire coral *Millepora* sp.

Symbiotic algae also supply most of the food for the common, brown-coloured soft corals, which, like the reef-building stony corals, also have zooxanthellae in their tissues. Many soft corals are supported by water pressure in special body cavities and can expand or contract in size quite rapidly. Some soft corals also have numerous small calcareous spicules in their bodies, which act as internal skeletons.

Mushroom soft corals *Sarcophyton* sp.

Because stony corals need light to drive the photosynthetic factories of their zooxanthellae, they must grow in shallow waters exposed to sunlight. Those in shaded positions usually die, so competition for a place in the sun can be intense. Many corals have a spreading growth form so that they can absorb as much sunlight as possible.

Above, left to right: Large polyps of the coral *Lobophyllia hemprichii*; Plate corals *Acropora hyacinthus*.

Many fast-growing corals have a growth form that lets them overgrow other corals and steal their space and sunlight. This competition may happen in slow motion, but it is no less fierce than the territorial disputes of terrestrial animals. Usually, these corals have no chemical defences and must rely on growing rapidly over their neighbours to outcompete them.

Whorl-forming colonies of Montipora aequituberculata.

Colonies in rich coral communities are constantly engaging their neighbours in a never-ending struggle for space, both for a place to grow and in order to gain access to light. Some corals have developed chemical defences to aid them in their highly competitive quest.

Pale brown clubs of *Acropora palifera* competing for space with spreading yellow-green sheets of *Porites lichen*.

THE WALL OF MOUTHS

Stony corals are not the only coral reef organisms that rely on symbiotic zooxanthellae for the bulk of their energy needs.

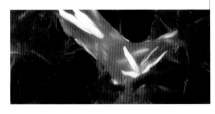

The common brown soft corals *Sarcophyton* and *Sinularia* are a major part of many reef communities and also host zooxanthellae in their tissues, as do some common sponges. Other groups of cnidarians, like the stinging fire corals, have zooxanthellae in their bodies, just like the "living fossil" blue corals (*Heliopora coerulea*), which have existed in their present form since the time of the dinosaurs. Even giant clams have more in common with plants than with other sea shells, spreading their colourful mantles to catch the light and feed the algae in their tissues. Reef-building stony corals, and all these other zooxanthellate reef animals, may only receive one-quarter of their food by trapping plankton animals from the surrounding water, but they are numerous on the Great Barrier Reef and they consume a lot of plankton.

Held up to the light, a sample of sea water fresh from the ocean may look clear, but under the microscope it is a teeming microcosm. Tiny bacteria and species of minute, single-celled plants called "phytoplankton" provide food for an array of microscopic animals collectively known as "zooplankton". Zooplankton includes the larvae of coral reef animals that spend time drifting in the ocean's currents before metamorphosing into miniature versions of their parents and finding a reef to live on. Many planktonic plants are so small that they pass easily through the finest plankton net. These diminutive "nanoplankton" remained unknown to science for years. Some planktonic animals, such as comb jellies and salps, are quite large but they are delicate, transparent and hard to see without the right angle of light. This community of unseen plants and animals forms the staple diet of many coral reef creatures.

Hundreds of the encrusting, filter-feeding animals living on coral reefs survive without symbiotic algae to supplement their planktonic food supply. These animals have opted for a more efficient lifestyle, or slow growth, enabling them to survive on the reef's naturally slim plankton pickings. Not having to rely on zooxanthellae has freed these animals from the light constraints shared by the many species with algal symbionts. Instead, they attach themselves to caves or on vertical walls and thrive in deep water where the sun fails to penetrate. Because their colour is not determined by algal pigment, many of these filter-feeders sport lurid patterns and brilliant colours. Bright reef sponges, fern-like stinging hydroids, huge gorgonian fans, yellow daisy corals, pink lace corals, towering black coral trees, multicoloured *Dendronephthya* soft corals, spiral Christmas tree worms and purple and yellow sea squirts are just some of the many planktonic filter-feeders common on coral reefs.

Other filter-feeding invertebrates are not attached to the bottom, preferring to move slowly from place to place. Crinoids, or feather stars, have multitudinous arms, each bearing fern-like pinnules covered in sticky cilia, which trap plankton animals and pass them down a groove in each arm to a central mouth. Many-armed basket stars emerge from the reef at night to spread out a net of finely branched arms that trap plankton from the passing water. Some sea cucumbers, or holothurians, have modified their feeding arms to form a fine, mesh net covered in sticky mucus. They spread this net up into the water and wait until it has collected its catch of plankton. They then push, in turn, each arm into a central mouth, scraping off its bounty of plankton-laden mucus.

The myriad filter-feeders that live on the reef's slopes have been likened to a "wall of mouths". Plankton organisms swept into the vicinity of a reef must run the gauntlet of this remorseless, ever-hungry community. Filter-feeders quickly deplete plankton from the sea above the reef, unless it is constantly replenished with fresh, plankton-laden water by current movements. As a result, healthy filter-feeding communities only develop on exposed, current-swept regions of the reef — usually on corners or in narrow passes between reefs that act to funnel water. An enclosed water mass, such as a reef lagoon or a sheltered bommie field (where there is minimal water movement), may always be in a state of partial plankton depletion. Such habitats normally do not support many filter-feeders. A good example of such depletion can be observed in sea caves. Filter-feeders abound on cave walls near the entrance, but further back in the darkness food levels rapidly drop-off and eventually the walls are bare — no food can negotiate the wall of mouths positioned around the outside of the cave.

Because plankton is often in short supply, many corals and other filter-feeders constantly compete for food. Some have adopted strategies to overcome food shortage. Those that can move, position themselves on high, current-swept vantages with unobstructed access to food. Sea whips, black corals and gorgonian fans adopt a high-growth form to elevate themselves above their neighbours, ensuring they are the first to receive an intake of fresh plankton. Sponges capture and feed on tiny nanoplankton and bacteria, which are too small for most other animals and are plentiful even when most large plankton has been filtered out of the water. Bryozoans also feed on the nanoplankton missed by most other filter-feeders, and have adopted growth and lifestyle strategies that minimise their energy requirements; consequently, they do not need much food to survive.

Attached benthic animals without symbiotic algae must get all of their energy from the plankton they trap from the surrounding water. These animals do not require sunlight. They can live in caves or overhangs and survive in deep water where there is not enough light for photosynthesis. Many of these animals are more brightly coloured than stony corals.

A large barrel sponge *Xestospongia testudinaria* surrounded by many colourful gorgonian species.

The densely packed polyps of this gorgonian each have eight tentacles covered in fine pinnules. The pinnules are covered in stinging cells, or "nematocysts", which trap plankton drifting past. Trapped plankton is passed into the mouth lying at the centre of these tentacles. It takes a lucky plankton animal to run this stinging gauntlet of tentacles.

Whip gorgonians *Ellisella* sp.

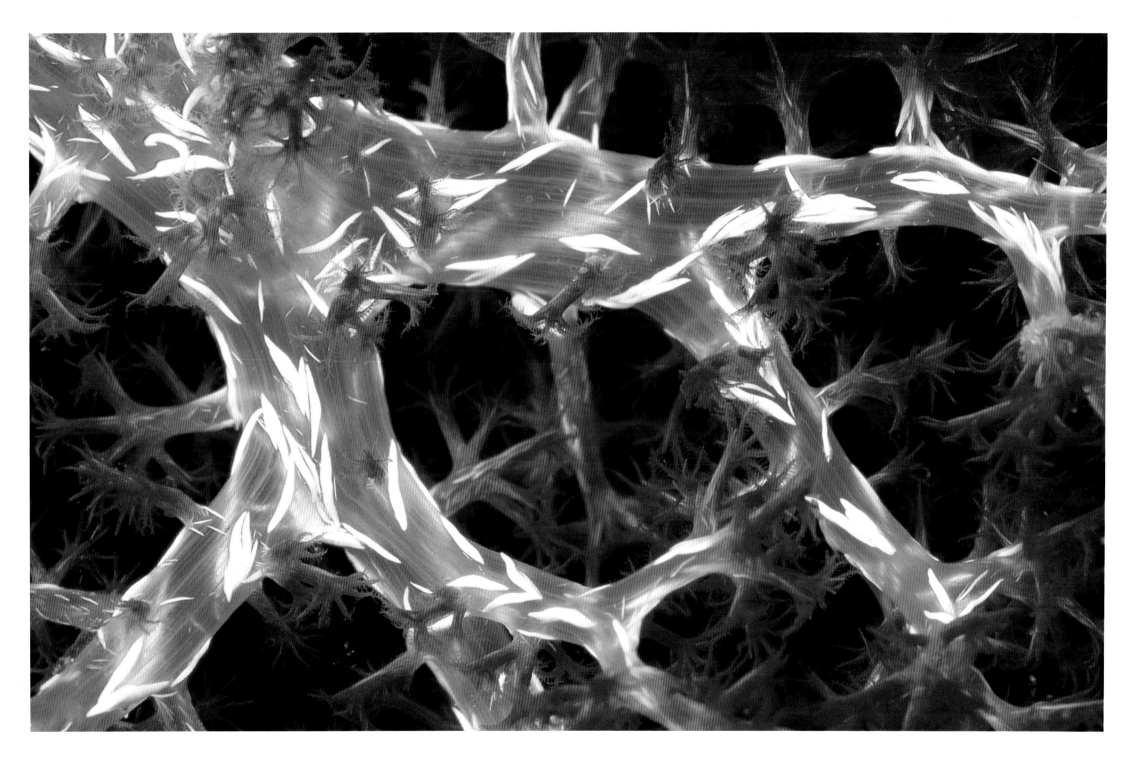

Many soft corals and gorgonians lack symbiotic algae, so they are able to grow in caves and on deep vertical walls where they use their clumps of brightly coloured polyps to trap plankton. Water pressure supports their tree-like branching colonies, which can grow to over 2 metres in height. Strength-giving white spicules can be seen in the translucent body.

Colourful *Dendronephthya* soft coral.

Plankton feeders do not require access to sunlight, but they do require plenty of plankton. Competition for food, rather than space, drives these animals and many have evolved supporting skeletons that help them grow well off the bottom and rise above other plankton feeders. Plankton is quickly depleted from still water and filter-feeders are most abundant in current-swept areas.

Above, left to right: A diver examines a huge *Dendronephthya* soft coral tree; Colourful soft corals and sponges on a deep reef wall.

Opposite: Large gorgonian fan, fan sponges *Ianthella basta* (centre) and *Dendronephthya* soft coral.

Thousands of years of coral growth and sculpting by waves and currents has created a maze of grottos, caves, tunnels and canyons on many coral reefs. This varied topography provides homes and shelter for a multitude of reef animals.

Prismatic light explodes on the shoulder of a deep reef canyon.

PLACES TO LIVE

The structure of living communities determines the range of environments that are available for animals and plants to inhabit. This is especially the case for coral reefs.

It has been estimated that there are more species of plants and animals in one cubic metre of the Great Barrier Reef than in any other environment in the world — including tropical rainforests! The myriad places to live within a coral reef range from caves and tunnels, to overhangs and cracks, to the narrow spaces among corals, to the surface and interior of the coral colonies themselves.

Caves, tunnels, overhangs and cracks in the reef provide shelter for many nocturnal animals during the day. Soldierfishes, sweepers and bigeyes drift quietly to and fro in these shelters while the sun is up, emerging at night to feed. Similarly, crayfish, slipper lobsters and crabs avoid the gaze of predators by hiding in deep cracks and crevices during the day, but under the cover of darkness they roam freely over the reef, searching for food. With the exception of those species that clean fishes for a living, shrimps are never seen on the reef during the day. At night, however, a diver's torch over the bottom reflects their glowing eyes and closer inspection reveals a variety of shrimp species resplendent in red or orange livery. Fantastic basket stars secrete themselves in cracks and caves during the day, resembling tangled masses of string. At night they emerge, unfold and become net-like plankton traps a metre wide.

Many other species occasionally rest or hide in caves and cracks. Predatory fish, such as coral trout, Queensland gropers, large cods, stripeys and mangrove jacks, often stake out caves, tunnels and overhangs. Sometimes they appear to be waiting in ambush for unsuspecting prey; at other times they seem to be simply resting. Even large sharks rest in caves. Whitetip reef sharks up to 2 metres long, and 3-metre-long tawny sharks, are frequently seen lying on the bottom of caves and tunnels. Coral rockcod (*Cephalopholis miniata*), moray eels and many other fishes live permanently in caves and spend most of their lives in these shelters. Amazing cleaner shrimps, which acquire all of their food by picking parasites, fungal patches and dead tissue from the skin, mouths and gills of fishes, also ply their trade from the shelter of cracks and holes in the reef.

Cowrie shells, cone shells and many other sea shells shelter beneath the bunkers of dead coral plates and boulders strewn over the surface of coral reefs, as do brittle stars and some species of sea urchins. Multifarious flatworms, polychaetes and other worms make their homes in the maze of interstices between dead and live coral colonies. Thousands of tiny amphipod and isopod species crawl over and among corals and other bottom-dwelling animals. Hundreds of other animal species burrow into the limestone of dead corals, seeking shelter and food within the matrix of the reef itself. Some of

these animals rasp the coral rock away to create their burrows, while others secrete acids that dissolve the limestone. Colourful Christmas tree worms have developed a unique way of burrowing into living coral colonies. A larval worm settles from the plankton onto the surface of a living *Porites* boulder coral, secreting a tiny protective tube. As the coral grows, the worm keeps pace, extending its tube so that it always stays just at the surface of the coral. Eventually, an adult worm will have a tube extending over 50 millimetres into the coral — and no burrowing effort was ever required!

Living corals are the abodes of many other reef animals. Branching corals have innumerable nooks and crannies that make ideal homes for species that are protected from the stinging cells of the corals. Almost every branching coral has resident small, colourful xanthid crabs. Scientists have found that the xanthid crab *Trapezia*, which is found only among the branches of *Pocillopora* corals, can sometimes keep the coral-eating crown-of-thorns sea star from eating its host by repeatedly nipping the tube feet of the approaching sea star.

The most unusual of the many crabs living among live corals is the coral gall crab (*Hapalocarcinus marsupialis*). Females of this species settle on the surface of a coral and somehow alter its growth pattern, so the coral grows around the crab, enclosing the canny crustacean within a 10-millimetre-wide cave with several small openings. The female crabs spend their entire lives inside these coral caves. Males are free-living and much smaller than females. When the time is right, they squeeze in through these tiny entrance holes to mate. Many small fish species are only found among the branches of living corals and rarely leave the home shelter of their chosen coral colony. The bright red and black patterned flame hawkfish (*Neocirrhites armatus*) spends its life living among the branches of a single *Pocillopora eydouxi* colony.

The bizarre pea crab spends its whole life hidden in the mantle cavity of a bivalve mollusc. A single male and female pair lives in a clam or mussel, feeding on particles of food filtered by their mollusc host. Different species of bivalves are home to many tiny species of crab that are never seen unless their host is killed and opened. One pea crab species is not so tiny. *Xanthasia murigera* makes its home only in the mantle cavity of the giant clam. This species has plenty of room to spread out and grows to about 20 millimetres across the carapace. Everywhere we turn on the Great Barrier Reef there are strange living habits and relationships that have evolved because of the remarkable high diversity and long-term stability of this amazing ecosystem.

These strikingly vibrant shrimps live in permanent pairs in caves and holes in the reef. Their long white antennae and bright colours advertise their services as cleaners of passing fishes. A bundle of green eggs can be seen held securely beneath the body of the larger female.

Banded coral shrimps *Stenopus hispidus* await passing customers.

Smaller elongate fangblennies make their living by sneaking quick bites from unsuspecting fishes as they swim past. During the breeding season, males prepare a nest in a hole in the reef and attract females, who lay eggs in the nest. The male then carefully guards the eggs until they hatch.

A bluestriped fangblenny *Plagiotremus rhinorhynchus* at the entrance to his nesting hole.

HABITATS

Every reef on the Great Barrier Reef is different, but even within individual coral reefs there is little homogeneity. Individual reefs are subdivided into a number of habitats that support unique collections of corals, fishes and other marine animals.

On any reef the richest habitats are usually found on the shallow front reef slope — especially at points and corners where the current sweeps around. Because the prevailing wind in the Great Barrier Reef region is the south-east trade wind, reefs are usually described in relation to this wind direction. Thus, the front of a reef is the south-east side, exposed to the full force of the trade winds, while the back reef is the more sheltered north-west side. The exposed front side of the reef is usually a solid rampart with a relatively steep slope — supporting a colourful community of corals and other encrusting animals, together with many fish species. The shallow part of the front slope, under perpetual barrage from breaking waves, is called the reef crest. Large swells in times of rough weather exert a constant, smashing force on the reef crest, so only strong, firmly cemented corals can survive. Some fishes have developed specialist lifestyles beneath the surge of breaking waves and exist only in these turbulent habitats.

As the back reef is protected from swell, it is usually a much gentler habitat. A complex maze of patch reefs and bommies often develops here, with a varied and labyrinthine topography. There are caves and tunnels to explore, as well as beautiful coral gardens with spires and domes, rippled white sand patches and fields of staghorn corals. The coral and fish communities are not usually as rich as on the front reef, but the diversity of species is often higher. An enclosed shallow lagoon sometimes develops along the back reef, with a mosaic of low coral patches on the sandy floor. Food is often in short supply in the lagoon and the water is more turbid than on the outside of the reef. Coral cover is usually low but many species prefer these sheltered conditions and are only common in this habitat. The young of some reef fish species spend their early lives in the safe waters of these lagoons and only venture out when they reach adult size.

On the deeper slopes of the reef, below 50 metres, lies the deep reef habitat. These are dangerous depths — divers risk the mind-altering distortion of nitrogen narcosis and decompression sickness (or the bends). Still, the fascinating allure of marine life in this habitat tempts many scientists to explore its secrets. Stony corals become rare and colourful sponges, sea whips, gorgonians and black coral trees grow in profusion. An entirely different group of fishes inhabit this gloomy realm. Most of these fishes are small and colourful and many have only been discovered and described over the past 30 years.

Some intrepid naturalists now use sophisticated, mixed-gas diving apparatus to push the frontiers of continental slope exploration beyond the realms of the true coral reef. This is the world of the chambered nautilus. This bizarre relative of the octopus and squid is a living fossil that has survived virtually unchanged for hundreds of millions of years. This ultra-deep reef habitat is 100–150 metres deep, but divers have found there is still enough light to see. Many of the fishes

and encrusting animals from these ultra-deep reefs have never before been seen by humans. Ultra-deep reef habitat is yet to be explored in the Great Barrier Reef region. Scientists can only speculate on what will be found on the deep front of the outer barrier reefs.

The Great Barrier Reef World Heritage Area is much more than coral reefs. Reefs make up only 5% of the region but they receive most of the scientific community's attention. Other habitats within the region may not be as spectacular or as diverse as coral reefs, but they too have many interesting and intriguing stories to tell. The Great Barrier Reef Marine Park's mass of open ocean is such a habitat. A unique community of pelagic creatures spend their entire lives in the blue waters of the Coral Sea. Sea jellies, such as the Portuguese man-o-war (or bluebottle), drift on the sea's surface, along with the blue sunbursts of *Porpita pacifico* jellies and the beautiful, blue floating nudibranchs *Glaucus atlanticus*. Vast schools of flyingfish feed on zooplankton near the surface, pursued by blue and yellow dolphinfish (or mahi mahi). Gigantic tuna and marlin patrol the void, along with whale sharks and one of the open ocean's most frightening predators — the oceanic whitetip shark. Pilot whales and deep-diving sperm whales are also open-ocean nomads that scour the light-less depths for squid.

Over the continental shelf lies the sandy inter-reef habitat and the more inshore Great Barrier Reef lagoon floor habitat. Both of these habitats have numerous small reef patches scattered across their (mostly) sandy floors. Free-living algae, sponges, corals, gorgonians and ascidians have all adapted well to life on open, sandy bottoms, as have a variety of sea cucumbers, feather stars, nudibranchs, sea urchins and sea stars. Several species of *Halophila* seagrass form sparse meadows at depths of 10–60 metres, and the calcareous green algae *Halimeda* grows in thick beds along the inside of the outer barrier reef. These beds have built up a loose reef of dead algae fragments, raising the growing surface more than 10 metres above the surrounding sea floor. Closer to the coast, at depths of less than 10 metres, dense seagrass meadows cover large areas of the shallow lagoon floor, creating a rich grazing ground for almost 15,000 dugongs. These placid relatives of the elephant feed exclusively on seagrasses and are extinct or severely endangered outside the protected Great Barrier Reef region.

Along the coast and around many of the islands of the Great Barrier Reef are extensive stands of mangroves. A total of 37 species of mangrove grow in this region, with several species reaching heights of 30 metres. A number of so-called mangrove islands on the northern inshore reef have stilt-rooted *Rhizophora* mangroves growing in impenetrable tangles on shallow reef flats, covering an area of many hectares and resisting all but the most severe cyclones.

A plethora of animals have become superbly adapted to life in the open ocean. Beautiful blue and silver Glaucus nudibranchs float upside down, crawling along on the surface film of the sea and swallowing air to stay afloat. These remarkable nudibranchs capture the nematocysts from the hydrozoans they eat, place these stinging cells in their long wing-like cerata, and then use them for their own defence.

The strange ocean-drifting nudibranch *Glaucus atlanticus* feeding on the floating hydrozoan *Porpita pacifico*.

Reefs are not all coral — large areas of sand are common in lagoonal and back reef habitats of the Great Barrier Reef. Shallow sand flats appear devoid of life but a close examination reveals a wealth of interesting animals, including many different hole-dwelling gobies. Shrimpgobies, such as these, have a symbiotic relationship with pairs of snapping shrimps. The gobies live in the shrimps' holes and provide an early warning system to counter any impending danger. In return, the shrimps maintain the burrow.

A pair of yellow shrimpgobies *Cryptocentrus cinctus.*

A feeding pair of crab-eye gobies
Signigobius biocellatus.

Diverse coral habitats on the reef support distinct species and growth forms of coral. In habitats regularly exposed to strong swells, the corals are stronger, grow lower and have a sturdier structure. Conversely, those corals in sheltered parts of the reef are more fragile and often have erect or branched growth forms.

A community of robust *Acropora* corals grows close to the bottom on a reef edge exposed to continuous swell.

In the blue depths below 50 metres, corals are rare but a variety of large plankton-feeding gorgonians and black coral trees are found. Colourful sponges and ascidians are also common in this deep reef habitat. Further down the slope from these depths, the water fades to black.

Above, left to right: *Ellisella* gorgonians on a deep reef slope; A diver investigates a huge black coral tree *Antipathes* sp.

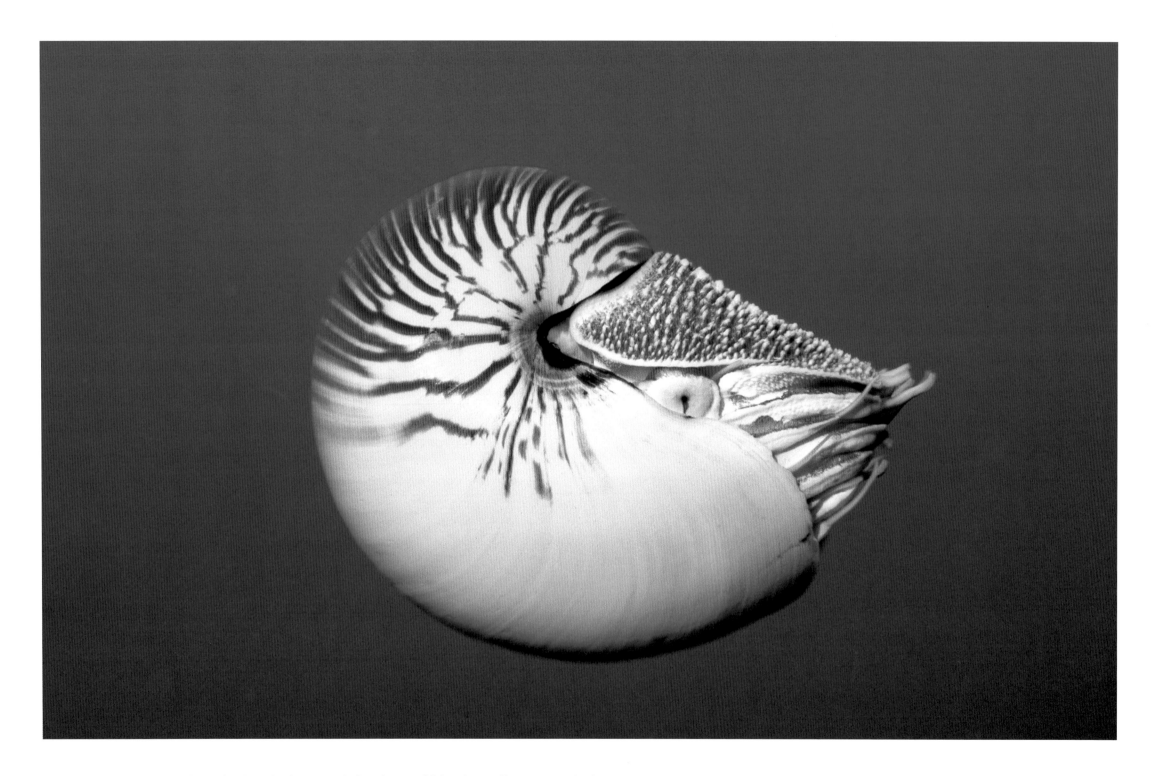

The chambered nautilus is a living fossil, a relic from times before the age of fishes (500 million years ago) when very similar ammonoids ruled the seas. Ammonites up to 2 metres in diameter were compatriots of the dinosaurs but all except a few small nautilus species have been relegated to prehistory. Nautiluses live on deep reef slopes at depths between 60–750 metres. They regulate their buoyancy by either increasing or decreasing the amount of air within the chambers of their shells.

A chambered nautilus *Nautilus pompilius* propels itself with jet-like bursts of water pumped through a large, moveable siphon on its body.

A suite of fishes that occupy the deep reef habitat are never seen in the sunlit habitats above. Small colourful wrasses, angelfishes, damselfishes and plankton-feeding fairy basslets are common in this realm, although their bright colours can only be fully appreciated when illuminated by a photographer's electronic flash.

Yellowback basslet *Pseudanthias bicolor.*

ABOVE THE WATER

Not all of the Great Barrier Reef World Heritage Area lies submerged beneath the water's surface. Many beaches, coral cays and high islands dot the region and form important habitats for their own plant and animal communities.

Beautiful, white sandy beaches front the Great Barrier Reef seas, but most are not composed from coral sand derived from the reef, but almost purely from silica sand of terrestrial origin. At first glance, the beaches may appear to be barren places, but in fact lots of animals make their homes, nests and shelters on these beaches. Swift ghost crabs roam the upper foreshore, ranging out from deep burrows in the sand. Smaller ghost crab species glean organic detritus from the littoral zone once the tide retreats, leaving an intriguing pattern of sand balls about the size of the crabs themselves. On the lower beach, sea snails and sand dollar urchins crawl just beneath the surface, leaving distinctive tracks across the wet sand. Piles of spaghetti-like sand castings mark the remains of a worm's meal. Soldier crabs emerge from the sand to feed on the lower beach as the tide retreats. As their name suggests, these crabs live in large battalions, feeding on detritus left on the sand's surface by the receding water. When danger threatens, soldier crabs quickly "corkscrew" beneath the sand.

Storm waves may accumulate coral sand and rubble on the back edge of a reef to form a small sand island or coral cay. Many reefs have cays but a lot of them only emerge from the water at low tide. Larger cays may remain permanently exposed and become vegetated over time — first with clumps of grass and later with shrubs and trees. Vegetated cays accumulate sand more rapidly and may become quite large, sometimes rising more than 10 metres above sea level.

Large vegetated cays are common in the Capricorn–Bunker group at the south end of the Great Barrier Reef and are also found scattered over the rest of the reef region. Marine turtles nest on cays and beaches throughout the World Heritage area. Because they are usually free of land predators, cays also become havens for nesting and roosting sea birds — a large cay may be home to more than 100,000 sea birds. Sooty, bridled and crested terns lay their eggs on the sand, gathering in large, closely packed colonies. Dark-coloured noddy terns build rudimentary nests of twigs and seaweed in shrubs and trees, while shearwaters (or muttonbirds) dig nesting burrows in the sand beneath. Raine Island, a vegetated coral cay on the far northern outer Great Barrier Reef, is the most famous of these bird-nesting cays. A total of 52 species of sea bird have been recorded on this tiny island, including species that nest nowhere else in the Great Barrier Reef region.

Dense stands of *Rhizophora* mangroves form "islands" on some northern inshore reefs. During the summer months, tens of thousands of Torresian imperial pigeons arrive from New Guinea to nest on these islands, which are safe from all predators. During their seven-month stay in the area to hatch their eggs and rear their young, these beautiful black and white pigeons take turns journeying to mainland rainforests to feed.

Hundreds of high islands also punctuate the Great Barrier Reef region. Most are simply "sample patches" of the mainland coast, with the addition of a few special coastal plants and animals. At the height of the last ice age these islands were all part of the mainland. Since then, over the past 10,000 years or so, they have all gradually become isolated from the mainland.

The Great Barrier Reef World Heritage Area includes many sand cays, small and large islands, and mainland beaches within its boundaries. Plenty of sand-dwelling invertebrate animals, nesting turtles and sea birds live on these beaches and cays, or use them during the breeding season.

Exposed beach and fringing reef encircles a small sand cay.

Mainland and island beaches within the Great Barrier Reef Marine Park frequently border terrestrial national parks, such as Whitsunday Island National Park shown above. The cross-over of such boundaries ensures the entire ecosystem remains in pristine condition and also controls land use in the coastal catchments.

Beautiful Whitehaven Beach and Hill Inlet in the Whitsunday Islands.

As the water recedes on the sand beaches and estuary flats of eastern Queensland, vast armies of soldier crabs emerge to feed on the organic detritus left by the tide. The crabs scoop up the surface layer of sand, eat the plant and animal debris and discard the rest. When danger threatens, these crabs rapidly disappear, spiralling down into the sand.

Clockwise from top left: A battalion of soldier crabs on the march; Soldier crab *Myctyris longicarpis*; These crabs can quickly vanish into the sand.

Remarkably, female turtles consistently return to the same beach (believed to be the beach of their own birth) to lay their eggs. At night, they laboriously haul themselves up the beach and dig a nesting hole in the sand above the tideline. Most females lay about 100 ping-pong-ball-sized eggs before covering their nests with sand and returning to the sea, often early the next morning. The eggs hatch about seven weeks later and the young turtles quickly scramble down to the sea.

Above, left to right: Female turtles lay a clutch of eggs in a shallow nest scooped in the sand; A female green turtle *Chelonia mydas* returns to the sea after laying her eggs.

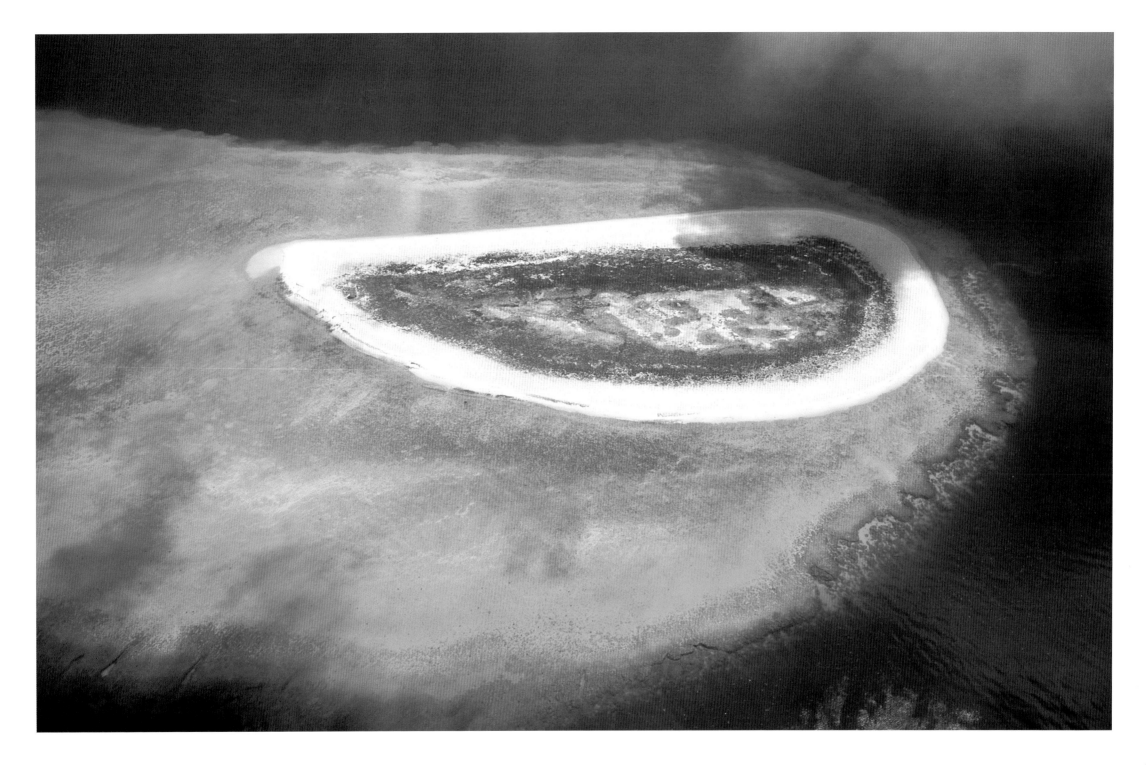

Every year in spring tens of thousands of green turtles gather around Raine Island — a small vegetated sand cay on the outer barrier reef near the tip of Cape York. During a big year, up to 14,000 females may nest on the beaches of this unique cay in a single night, making it the most important green turtle rookery in the world.

Opposite: Green turtles *Chelonia mydas* gather to breed at Raine Island.

Above: Raine Island on the northern Great Barrier Reef.

Offshore cays are free from terrestrial predators, making them important sea bird nesting sites. A large cay may support more than a quarter of a million sea birds of various species. Terns, noddy terns, boobies, herons and shearwaters are the most abundant bird groups. Tropicbirds, red-footed boobies and frigatebirds nest only on Raine Island in the Great Barrier Reef region.

Heron Island, a vegetated cay in the Capricorn–Bunker Group at the southern end of the Great Barrier Reef.

Clockwise from top left: Red-footed boobies *Sula sula* nesting on Raine Island; Black noddy *Anous minutus* with chick; Courting wedge-tailed shearwaters *Puffinus pacificus*; Masked booby *Sula dactylatra* pair with chick on a sand cay beach.

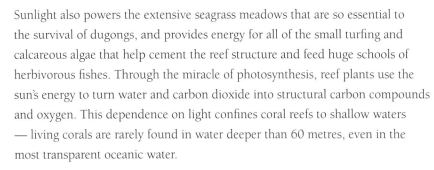

THE WEB OF LIFE

All of the energy that powers the community of the Great Barrier Reef ultimately comes from the sun. Sunlight drives the symbiotic algal factories that feed all reef-building corals and fuels the plant plankton that sustains vast hordes of animal plankton, which, in turn, become food for the reef's many filter-feeders.

Sunlight also powers the extensive seagrass meadows that are so essential to the survival of dugongs, and provides energy for all of the small turfing and calcareous algae that help cement the reef structure and feed huge schools of herbivorous fishes. Through the miracle of photosynthesis, reef plants use the sun's energy to turn water and carbon dioxide into structural carbon compounds and oxygen. This dependence on light confines coral reefs to shallow waters — living corals are rarely found in water deeper than 60 metres, even in the most transparent oceanic water.

In terrestrial ecosystems, plants are a dominant feature of the terrain — grasses, shrubs and trees make up the bulk of visible life. Plants are all but invisible on a coral reef, but only because most plant plankton is microscopic and billions of symbiotic algae are hidden within the bodies of reef animals. Similarly hard to see are turfing algae, which form a near-invisible fuzz on the surface of dead coral, and the pink coralline algae that cements the reef structure and merges seamlessly with the reef rock. The only visible plants on most offshore reefs are patches of bright green turtle weed and a few clumps of large red algae. Coastal fringing reefs may have a forest of large *Sargassum* algae in the upper few metres, but most reefs have no algal forests at all.

If plants are not visible on most coral reefs how does the energy from the sun get transferred up the food chain? On coral reefs, the boundary between plant and animal is not always clearly defined. Is a stony coral or a giant clam a plant or an animal? More than half of their energy needs come from the sun via symbiotic zooxanthallae and reef animals would die without these crucial algae. The best way of examining this conundrum is to regard most zooxanthellate reef animals as herbivores that obtain the bulk of their energy from plants without having to eat them. Most of these animals supplement this efficient herbivorous lifestyle with carnivorous feeding on planktonic snacks.

Many animals on the reef are true herbivores, grazing on algae or other plants for their energy needs. Crustaceans, such as crabs and rock lobsters, graze on algae, as do trochus snails and sea slugs such as the sea hare *Aplysia*. However, most obvious herbivores on coral reefs are fishes and many different groups have adopted a largely herbivorous lifestyle, feasting on the rich, ever-replenished lawn of turf algae that coats all dead coral. Like most terrestrial herbivores (such as cows and sheep) herbivorous fishes spend most of their time eating, head down, scraping or nipping at the algal lawn. Many of the smaller herbivorous fishes, such as the damselfishes and the beautiful bluelined surgeonfish *Acanthurus lineatus,* guard their own private algal gardens so that they always have access to a lush supply of food. Even when hundreds of large grazers descend on their patch, these territorial defenders refuse to submit — battering intruders until they retreat to a less-fortified section of reef. As their name suggests, parrotfishes have fused teeth that form parrot-like beaks. Within their jaws, these fish have developed an incredibly powerful lever mechanism that enables them to scrape the surface off coral rocks and ingest turf algae growing on it (rather than just nipping off the tops of the tiny algal fronds). Parrotfishes also have strong grinding plates in their throats that help them crunch up fragments of coral rock. The giant bumphead parrotfish has such large, powerful jaws that it is able to feed on living coral as well as on the more porous coral rock. It can bite large chunks from live boulder corals, an extraordinary feat that is hard to replicate even with a chisel and sledgehammer.

Most of the so-called herbivores on the reef actually eat a mixture of algae and animal material. Algal grazers swallow huge numbers of tiny crustaceans that live among the algal turf, as well as encrusting animals such as sponges and ascidians. All fish herbivores rely on many species of symbiotic gut bacteria to help ferment and digest the algae and other food they eat. This is another example of the importance of symbiotic relationships in the coral reef ecosystem. The unique *Epulopiscium* gut bacteria, discovered in the gut of some surgeonfish, are thousands of times larger than most other bacteria. They may reach a length of over half a millimetre and be visible to the naked eye.

Other types of grazers — with no equivalent in terrestrial ecosystems — play a crucial role in the coral reef ecosystem. These animals graze on the various types of encrusting animals that dominate much of the reef community. Corals, soft corals, sponges, bryozoans and ascidians are attached to the bottom and cannot escape predation. Although many of them are toxic or hard to eat, specialist invertebrate grazers have developed ways to take advantage of their prey's immobility. Flatworms, sea spiders, sea shells and sea stars all feed on these encrusting animals, but nudibranchs are the true specialists in this lifestyle. A fantastic array of colourful nudibranchs feed on sponges, soft corals and other encrusting invertebrates. Those that feed on sponges manage to remove the spicules (glass-like shards found in sponges) without ever damaging their gut. Incredibly, they can even isolate the sponge toxins and store them in their own tissues for defence!

Some fishes are specialist grazers on encrusting animals, including the colourful angelfishes that eat sponges and ascidians. Before any food is swallowed, it is coated with mucus to protect the gut lining from any sharp spicules. Many of the brightly patterned butterflyfishes feed on mucus secreted by stony corals and are totally dependent on coral colonies for their food. These are just a few of the many examples of specialised and unusual lifestyles among coral reef organisms.

Large algae or seaweeds are not found on offshore reefs of the Great Barrier Reef, but can form forests in shallow water on fringing reefs. Short turfing algae covers all dead coral on offshore reefs and provides abundant food for herbivorous fishes; a few larger algae also live on these reefs. Large areas of shallow sandy habitat close to the coast are covered by seagrass meadows, which are also sometimes found across deeper inter-reef habitats. Estuaries throughout the Great Barrier Reef region are lined with mangrove forests, which also grow around offshore cays and islands and sometimes form "mangrove islands" on coastal reefs in the northern region of the marine park.

Clockwise from top left: Dull green club-shaped branches of the alga *Caulerpa racemosa* among flattened bright green discs of *Halimeda* sp.; Stilt roots of the red mangrove *Rhizophora stylosa* surrounded by seagrasses; Silt-covered fronds of the seagrass *Cymodocea rotundata*.

Many reef invertebrates consume the turf algae that covers all dead coral on the reef. Crabs, lobsters, sea hares and most sea snails are herbivores that feed on this unlimited resource.

Spotted reef crab *Carpilius maculatus*.

Algal turf, which covers all dead coral, makes a nutritious meal for herbivorous reef fishes. Many damselfishes, as well as most parrotfishes, surgeonfishes, unicornfishes and rabbitfishes, are herbivores that rely on this turf (and the small animals and organic matter contained within it) for their food. All of these fishes have a gut full of special symbiotic bacteria that helps them ferment and digest the algae they eat.

A male bignose unicornfish *Naso vlamingi* flashes his courting colours.

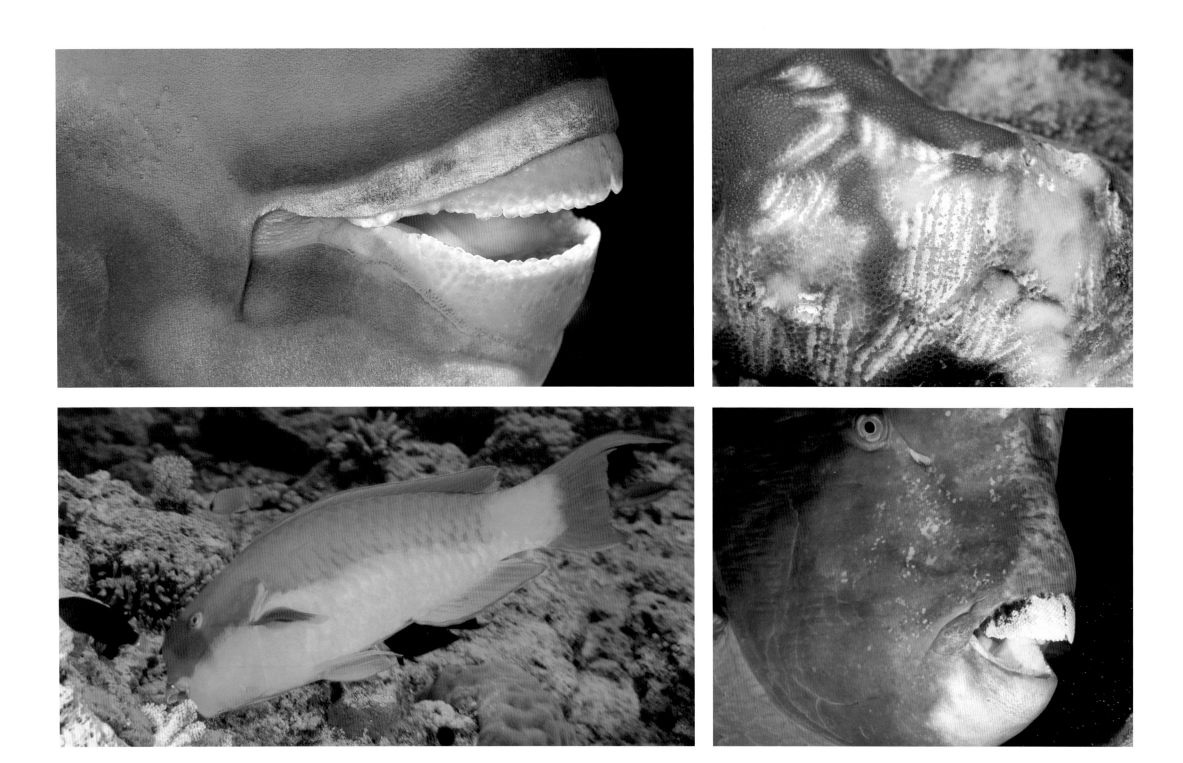

Parrotfishes in the family Scaridae are the most abundant of the reef's large herbivorous fishes. Sharp, fused teeth in a parrot-like beak, coupled with a lever-action jaw mechanism, support the parrotfish's extremely powerful bite. Rather than simply cropping off the algal turf, parrotfishes scrape off part of the dead coral beneath — ensuring they consume all available turf and any organisms living within. Like most herbivores, parrotfishes spend the bulk of their day feeding.

Clockwise from top left: A parrotfish's teeth are fused into a parrot-like beak; Tell-tale parrotfish bites on *Porites* coral; The powerful beak of the bumphead parrotfish *Bolbometopon muricatum*; Steephead parrotfish *Chlorurus microrhinos* grazing on algal turf.

Bumphead parrotfish are the giants of the parrotfish family and can reach 1.5 metres in length and weigh 50 kilograms. They often travel in schools that can number over 100 individuals. Bumpheads are the only parrotfish species to ingest chunks of live corals as a major part of their diet, and consequently do a lot of damage to coral communities. Powerful grinding plates in their throats reduce the coral and turf they eat to a fine paste, which is fermented in the gut with special bacteria to aid digestion. Parrotfishes produce much of the sand found on coral reefs because their faeces are mainly fine coral sand.

A school of bumphead parrotfish *Bolbometopon muricatum*. Individual fish consume around a cubic metre of living coral every year.

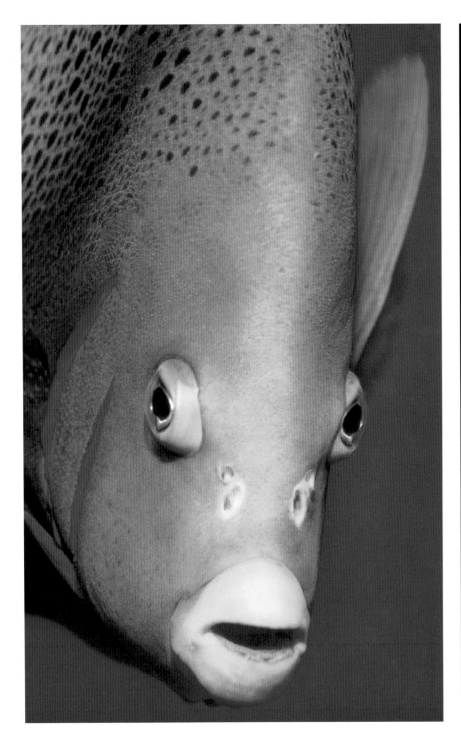

Angelfishes are among the most vivid of all the reef fishes. Small mouths and powerful jaws make them suited to a diet of sponges and other encrusting animals, which they scrape from the walls of tunnels and caves where they spend a lot of their time. Angelfishes are the noisiest reef fishes and can make a remarkably loud drumming sound when alarmed.

Above, left to right: Blue angelfish *Pomacanthus semicirculatus;* Threespot angelfish *Apolemichthys trimaculatus.*

Butterflyfishes either peck at the mucus produced by living corals or use their pointed snouts to pick small crustaceans from the reef. The beaked coralfish is an invertebrate picker, while the other species shown here are coral feeders. Because they are dependant on living corals, many of these beautiful fishes die whenever corals are destroyed by cyclones or crown-of-thorns sea stars.

Clockwise from top left: Chevron butterflyfish
Chaetodon trifascialis; Beaked coralfish
Chelmon rostratus; Blackbacked butterflyfish
Chaetodon melannotus; Mertens' butterflyfish
Chaetodon mertensii.

The brilliant colours of most nudibranchs are warning signals, advertising that these invertebrates are nasty to eat. Nudibranchs eat encrusting animals (such as sponges) and incorporate any toxins into their own bodies. Most nudibranchs are very fast-growing — even the Spanish dancer, the largest of them all, lives for less than a year. They are usually rare but have highly variable population numbers. At a certain time and place one species may become very common, but later may not be seen for years. Divers should make the most of every nudibranch sighting.

Above: Painted dorid nudibranch *Chromodoris coi.*

Opposite: Spanish dancer *Hexabranchus sanguineus.*

PREDATORS

Once energy from the sun has been transferred from algae to herbivores, it is the predators' turn to shift it further up the food chain. Coral reef predators — from compact, plankton-gulping damselfishes to hulking, man-eating tiger sharks — employ a fascinating spectrum of feeding strategies.

Planktivores come in a range of shapes and sizes and comprise one of the largest groups of coral reef predators. Feather stars, ancient relatives of the sea stars and sea urchins, spread pinnate (or feather-like) arms into the current to capture zooplankton. Tiny, mucus-covered cilia trap planktonic animals and pass them down a groove in each arm to the central mouth. Slender garden eels emerge from holes in the sand to pluck plankton from the surrounding water. Dense schools of baitfish and fusiliers constantly swallow plankton, relying on speed and sheer weight of numbers to avoid other predators. Larger fishes, such as the bigeye seabream and milkfish, also gulp plankton for their food, as do placid manta rays and giant whale sharks, which feed exclusively on plankton.

Plankton-eaters are rare in lagoons and other protected habitats where currents do not flow, but become so numerous around exposed reef edges that, unless currents regularly replenish supplies, they quickly deplete their food supply. When planktonic pickings are meagre and the water movement is too slow to bring in a worthwhile supply of food, small damselfishes shelter in the coral, not bothering to feed at the risk of exposing themselves to predation by larger fishes. Conversely, larger fishes, such as fusiliers, will swim several kilometres from one end of a reef to the other when the tide changes, in order to feed on the up-current end of the reef where plankton has not been depleted by the "wall of mouths".

A suite of reef predators feed on the abundant small crustaceans and invertebrates (such as molluscs and worms) that live on and among the algal and animal growth on the bottom. Most of these predators have small mouths and sharp canine teeth at the front of the jaw to make it easier to prise small animals from their hiding places. Pointed, elongate snouts, such as those sported by the birdnose wrasse and the beaked coralfish, help many invertebrate predators extract their prey from small cracks and holes. The hundred-odd species of wrasse that dwell on the Great Barrier Reef all have an invertebrate picking lifestyle, as do hawkfishes, monocle breams and dottybacks.

Some invertebrates are themselves efficient predators. Squids and cuttlefishes have extraordinary vision, speed and manoeuvrability (not to mention intelligence) to rival the skill set of any fish. These cephalopods also have the added advantage of ten arms, covered in gripping suction discs, which can shoot out to ensnare their prey. Fishes, crabs and shrimps all fall prey to these unusual, highly modified molluscs. Octopuses are also voracious coral

reef predators. They roam the reef, inserting their long mobile arms into cracks and crevices to flush out small fishes and crustaceans, which they wrangle in their powerful limbs and subdue with bites from their sharp, parrot-like beaks. Predatory groupers and cod often follow octopuses as they forage across the reef, opportunistically lunging at prey that escapes the octopus's deadly embrace. Octopuses mostly ignore their fishy entourage and continue to probe for food, flashing waves of shimmering colour over their bodies if excited.

At the top of the food chain are the piscivores — fishes that prey on other fishes. Most piscivores have gripping (rather than cutting teeth) and swallow their prey whole. Large mouths and throats, and expandable stomachs, allow them to accommodate any size fish they manage to swallow. Piscivores have adopted a variety of lifestyles to help them catch highly mobile and wary prey. The cunning sabre-toothed blenny, which mimics certain cleaner wrasses in order to boldly plunder the flesh of its trusting victims, is a specialized coral reef piscivore. Lizardfishes, wobbegong sharks and most scorpionfishes are ambush predators, lying motionless and camouflaged on the bottom. When an unsuspecting fish strays near, they erupt — engulfing their prey in an eye-blink. Other fishes, such as groupers and cod, are opportunistic predators. They swim slowly around, or rest on the bottom in full view, waiting for any inattentive fish that is distracted by other reef activity. The opportunist picks its target then makes a lightning-fast strike — ignoring other fishes that may be closer in range. Most feeding attempts are unsuccessful, but these predators simply wait patiently for more opportunities to present themselves.

Without doubt, the most dramatic predators are the pelagic fishes and sharks, which overwhelm their prey with sheer pace. These predators are always on the go, cruising the reef and inciting general fear wherever they roam. Fast-swimming pelagics (such as trevallies, mackerel, barracuda and tuna) are truly formidable predators and most reef fish scatter or dive frantically for shelter the moment any of these feared carnivores appear. They often hunt in groups and may herd baitfish into tight schools before launching frequent, murderous assaults into their midst. Some species of shark are fast enough to chase down most other fishes. Being the only piscivores to tear apart their prey, sharks are able to engage huge quarry. However, sharks are low-energy machines and their feeding opportunities are usually few and far between. Divers rarely see sharks attack — these apex predators spend most of their time in an efficient, cruising mode, waiting for that perfect moment to strike.

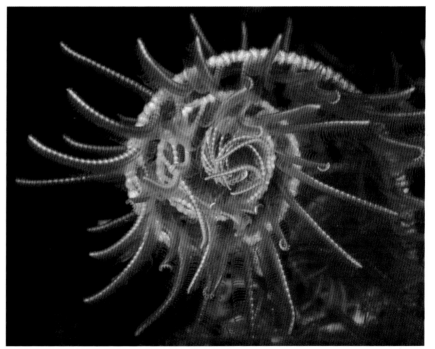

Feather stars, or crinoids, are filter-feeding echinoderms that are relatives of sea stars and sea urchins. This ancient group remains very similar to their forebears, which inhabited seas during the Ordovician period almost 500 million years ago. Feather stars are found on every available perch on coral reefs, extending their arms into the current to trap plankton animals on the fine mucus-covered cilia that line each pinnule on their many-segmented arms. Trapped food passes down a groove in each arm on its way along a conveyor belt of cilia toward the central mouth.

Clockwise from left: Feather star *Oxycomanthus* sp.; Feather star, possibly *Reometra* sp. on encrusting sponge; The coiled tip of a feather star arm *Comaster* sp. showing pinnules covered with plankton-trapping cilia.

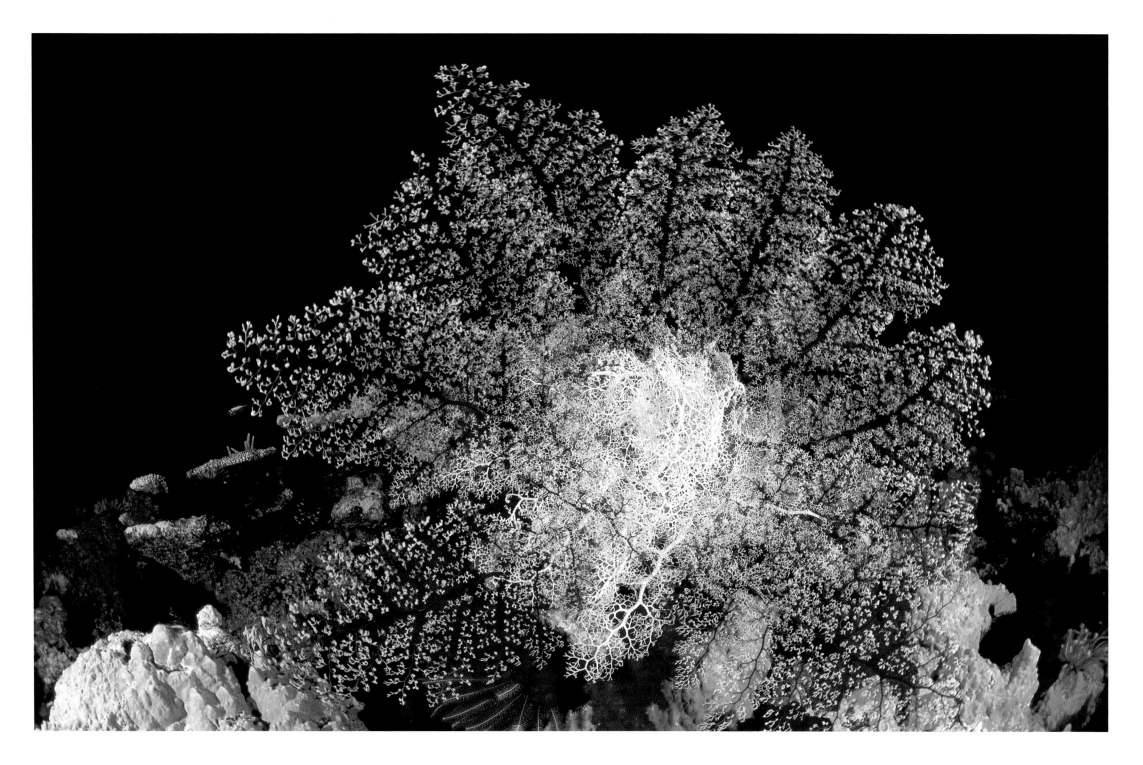

By day, basket stars resemble a tangled mass of string concealed deep within a crevice or cave. By night, they emerge to spread a net of plankton-trapping arms (spanning over a metre) into the current. The beautiful, spiral tentacle crowns of Christmas tree worms are also delicate plankton filters, which trap food and pass it down to the mouth at the base of the tentacles. These worms have rudimentary eyes, so if movement is detected the tentacle crown is quickly retracted to avoid a nip by a hungry fish. Amazingly, they can quickly grow another tentacle crown if such a mishap occurs.

Above: A basket star *Astroboa nuda* feeding at night.

Opposite: A group of Christmas tree worms *Spirobranchus giganteus* on a *Porites* coral colony.

Plankton is truly the quintessential sustenance of the sea. Small fishes such as damselfishes and fairy basslets pick individual plankton animals from the water with quick gulps of their extensible mouths. The world's largest fish, the 15-metre-long whale shark, is also a plankton feeder, swimming open-mouthed through the water and filtering out plankton and small fishes engulfed in its gigantic maw.

Above, left to right: Blackaxil pullers *Chromis atripectoralis* and orange basslets *Pseudanthias* cf. *cheirospilos*; The plankton-gulping mouth of a male mirror basslet *Pseudanthias pleurotaenia.*

Opposite: The whale shark *Rhincodon typus* is one of the reef's most majestic planktivores.

Fish species that feed by picking small invertebrates, such as crustaceans, sea snails and worms, from among the bottom growth usually have a set of sharp canine teeth at the front of their mouths to enable them to nip at their chosen prey. Because these teeth are not suited to cutting, these fishes have a set of crushing "pharyngeal" teeth in their throats to grind up food.

The striking harlequin tuskfish *Choerodon fasciatus* has a set of pronounced blue "picking" teeth, which turn pink whenever this fish feels threatened.

Octopuses, cuttlefishes and squids may only be highly evolved sea snails, but they have exceptional eyesight and long suckered arms that help rank them among the most effective predators on the reef. All these cephalopods have the ability to change colour instantly and can shimmer waves of colour across their bodies to reflect excitement or danger.

Above, left to right: Broadclub cuttlefish *Sepia latimanus*; Reef octopus *Octopus cyanea*.

Piscivores, such as this coral trout, usually have a number of large, sharp teeth to firmly grasp their struggling prey. Coral trout are opportunistic predators, roaming slowly around the reef and waiting for their quarry to come within range of their lightning-fast attack. They sometimes gather in groups to hunt schooling fishes.

The business end of the common coral trout *Plectropomus leopardus.*

Moray eels are fearsome predators that hide in holes, patiently waiting for unwary fish to venture near. Like most predators moray eels can expand their mouths and throats to swallow large prey if necessary. Morays have large canine teeth that lock firmly upright should the fish they capture protest too vigorously. These teeth can also fold backwards — making it easier to swallow subdued prey.

An undulate moray *Gymnothorax undulatus* swallowing an eyeline surgeonfish *Acanthurus nigricauda*.

Predatory fishes that regularly eat other fishes are known as piscivores. Piscivores range from small lurking lizardfishes (with large underslung jaws lined with needle sharp teeth) that spend most of their time lying patiently on the bottom, to fast-swimming schooling trevallies (or jacks) that roam in open water hunting smaller schooling fishes such as hardyheads and fusiliers.

Opposite: Variegated lizardfish
Synodus variegatus.

Above: School of bigeye trevally
Caranx sexfasciatus.

During the day many of the Great Barrier Reef's predatory fishes are found in resting schools. At night they disperse to feed, either around the reef itself or over the surrounding sandy habitats.

Above, left to right: A school of bluestriped snapper *Lutjanus kasmira*; Hussars *Lutjanus adetii* swimming in a school.

Large schools of tiny silvery baitfish are often found around reefs in the southern part of the Great Barrier Reef. At times these schools may surround a diver so tightly that it becomes impossible to see. Predatory fish have a field day with these baitfish and gather in large numbers to feed on the plentiful bounty.

A diver watches a pair of hussar *Lutjanus adetii* hunting schooling baitfish.

Not all sharks are fast-swimming, streamlined ocean wanderers. Many are camouflaged lurking predators, such as wobbegongs, which rest on the bottom waiting for unwary victims to stray within their range. Wobbegongs explode off the bottom in a rapid lunge, seizing their prey in strong jaws lined with small sharp teeth.

A tasselled wobbegong *Eucrossorhinus dasypogon* at rest.

Reef sharks are attracted by the sounds and smells of fish in distress and quickly congregate around spearfishers and their wounded catch. Sharks excited in this way have occasionally been known to bite divers that move too close to the action.

Whitetip reef sharks *Triaenodon obesus* circle a bait.

FISH AGES

Marine scientists have long known that it is possible to tell the age of a fish by counting the annual rings in its ear bones — in the same way that botanists can age trees by counting the rings in their trunks.

Over the past decade the ages of Great Barrier Reef fishes have been established using this process. As a result, we are beginning to understand the lifestyles of some Great Barrier Reef fishes. Some fish species stop growing when they reach adult size, as humans do. Other fish species undergo indeterminate growth and grow larger with every year of life. Most groupers and cod, as well as the commercially important coral trout, all continue to grow as they age, as do most wrasses and parrotfishes. Surgeonfishes, butterflyfishes and damselfishes, on the other hand, maintain a constant size as adults and it is impossible to estimate how old they are from size alone.

Fishes have a wide variety of different lifestyles. Some tiny gobies and small wrasses live, reproduce and die in less than a year — others are extremely long lived. Some deepwater Australian fishes do not become adults until they are 20–30 years old and live to 100–200 years of age. The black scalyfin, a temperate reef damselfish smaller than 20 centimetres long as an adult, lives for more than 100 years. It is interesting to imagine the changes that this long-lived territorial fish experiences as it goes about its life on the small patch of reef that it calls home. Other fishes come and go, algal forests die and regrow — even the reef structure changes — but the black scalyfin endures for four human generations.

At the other extreme of fish lifestyles on the Great Barrier Reef are the annual fishes, which grow quickly, lay their eggs and then die. The finespot wrasse (*Cirrhilabrus punctatus*) and the bluehead wrasse (*Thalassoma amblycephalum*) have both evolved a short lifestyle of rapid growth as the optimum way to survive in the diverse coral reef environment. These plankton-picking fishes are very common wherever currents provide plenty of food to support their frantic lifestyle. Fishes with this type of lifestyle often have dramatic "boom or bust" fluctuations in their populations because they are dependent on the conditions that their larvae encounter during the planktonic stage of their lives. When planktonic food for the larvae is plentiful there follows a corresponding boom in adult numbers a few months later. When planktonic food is scarce, only a few larvae survive and adult numbers decrease.

In between are a range of fishes that live to medium ages of 5–20 years — including the coral trout, which lives for 10–15 years, and many small damselfishes that are less than 10 centimetres long and also live remarkably

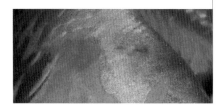

long lives of 15–20 years. The metre-long giant sweetlip (*Plectorhinchus albovittatus*) lives for 15–20 years as well. Size is no indicator of age — the beautiful 30-centimetre-long bluelined surgeonfish (*Acanthurus lineatus*) lives more than 50 years, but a 2-metre-long giant humphead Maori wrasse may only be 35 years old. The current Methuselah of coral reef fishes is the beautiful emperor angelfish (*Pomacanthus imperator*), which lives to an age of 70–80 years.

Long-lived fishes do not suffer the frequent population fluctuations of short-lived species and they are usually less common. Long-lived fishes still spawn every year, but over a period of 20 years or more they only need to have a few successful larval recruits to keep up their numbers. As a result, adult numbers are not affected by fluctuations in plankton conditions.

Most sharks take 8–15 years to reach maturity and live for a total of 25–50 years. Researchers can age sharks by counting annual rings in their vertebrae, in much the same way as counting growth rings in a tree trunk. Because sharks grow slowly and only produce a few young in their lifetime, most shark fisheries lack long-term sustainability.

The grey reef shark *Carcharhinus amblyrhyncos* can live for 20–30 years.

Fish ages vary enormously. At one extreme the reef pygmy goby grows to maturity and reproduces in less than two months; at the other extreme, some deepwater southern Australian fishes, such as the orange roughy and black oreo dory, may live for more than 150 years. A large humphead Maori wrasse may be over 35 years old and the oldest Great Barrier Reef fish aged so far, an angelfish, was about 80 years old.

The humphead Maori wrasse *Cheilinus undulatus* lives to a ripe old age of around 35 years.

The colourful Thalassoma *wrasses are short-lived coral reef fishes that expend their lives in one or two frantic years. Size is no indication of age in fishes and an 8-centimetre-long lemon damsel may be 20–30 years old, whereas a metre-long coral trout may be less than 10 years old. Coral trout are relatively short-lived, taking only one or two years to reach adulthood and living only 10–15 years at the most.*

Opposite: Surge wrasse *Thalassoma purpureum.*

Above: Common coral trout *Plectropomus leopardus.*

The largest of the parrotfishes, reaching a maximum length of around 1.3 metres, the bumphead parrotfish enjoys moderate longevity. Large adults have been aged at more than 40 years by scientists counting annual growth rings in their tiny ear bones.

Bumphead parrotfish *Bolbometopon muricatum.*

Large Pomacanthus *angelfishes are the oldest of the reef fishes aged to date. A 40-centimetre-long blueface angelfish may be 80 years old. Researchers have not yet found a reef fish that lives for more than 100 years of age, although a number of temperate water fish species may become centenarians.*

Blueface angelfish *Pomacanthus xanthometopon* with common cleanerfish *Labroides dimidiatus.*

PROTECTIVE STRATEGIES

Over the many millions of years that coral reef animals have lived together they have developed a multitude of fascinating protective strategies to lend them an edge in the dangerous dance of life. One of the most basic and enduring strategies is toxicity.

Possessing poison certainly discourages predation, but it never completely guarantees safety. Some predators have developed ways to isolate toxic substances and avoid their effects. Nevertheless, for the many reef creatures unable to swiftly evade predation, toxicity remains the best defence. Many sponges have toxins in their tissues, so too do ascidians and holothurians. All the cnidarians have toxic stinging cells (called "nematocysts"), which can be used both to capture planktonic food and deter grazers. Stony corals, soft corals, hydroids, gorgonians, black corals and tube anemones all use nematocysts to sting and discourage potential predators. The stings from many of these species are painful or irritating to humans and have a similar effect on most fishes.

Many invertebrate grazers that have evolved strategies to deal with the toxins of sponges, and other encrusting organisms, have also learned how to incorporate the poisons of the food they eat into their own tissues. Brightly coloured nudibranchs blatantly advertise the fact that they are full of sickening sponge poisons and are not nice to eat. Flatworms and sea spiders also accumulate sponge toxins and use vivid colours to warn predators away.

Some nudibranchs take the extraction of useful items from their food to amazing lengths. The giant aeolid nudibranch (*Phyllodesmium longicirra*) manages to eat its soft coral prey without triggering the stinging cells of the coral's polyps. It then moves the stinging cells to the ends of the long lobes (called "cerata") on its back, where they are utilised for its own defence. Not only does this nudibranch gain a means of defence, but it also incorporates the zooxanthellae from the soft coral into sacs in its own cerata. Here, the zooxanthellae live comfortably and provide some food for their new host.

Toxic chemicals called "holothurins" in the skin and body parts of sea cucumbers are coupled with another defence that is guaranteed to deter predators. When these holothurians are sufficiently disturbed, they eject a dense mass of sticky threads known as "cuvierian organs" from around the anus. These cuvierian organs are both sticky and toxic. A fish blanketed in poisonous sticky threads will quickly find its dinner unappetising.

Some fish groups are renowned for the poison used to protect themselves from predation. Pufferfishes are slow-swimming and have no protective spines but are eschewed by predators due to the powerful toxin contained in some of their organs. The infamous fugu is the stuff of legend in Japan. Qualified fugu chefs have been specially trained to remove the poisonous organs from these prized pufferfish. The delicious flesh can then be savoured by diners who readily part with their hard-earned yen to experience the giddy thrill of culinary Russian roulette. Unfortunately, in nature there is no such intermediary. Any fish that makes the fatal mistake of eating a pufferfish will quickly perish.

Armour or spines can also constitute effective protection from predators. Stony coral polyps encase themselves in limestone armour, and sea stars are covered in heavy calcareous nodules that are about as palatable as concrete. Sea urchins have made protection an art form. Their bodies are encased in a hard calcareous shell (called a "test") that is covered in sharp spines. The *Diadema* urchins — common on some Great Barrier Reef inshore reefs — have slender spines up to 20 centimetres long that they wave toward inquisitive predators. These urchins employ light-detecting organs, so whenever they sense movement lots of sharp spines bristle toward the intruder. However, this phalanx of spines fails to deter titan triggerfish determined to make a meal of urchin roe. Triggerfish smash their way through the spines, ignore the spikes penetrating their tough lips, and break into the test with their powerful jaws.

Most sea urchins harbour an irritant poison at the tips of their spines. As the name suggests, the crown-of-thorns sea star is well protected by toxic spines. The entire top of its body disc and its eighteen stubby arms are covered with a dense palisade of sharp, poisonous spines. A diver unfortunate enough to bump against a crown-of-thorns will testify to the toxicity of their spines. The pain is excruciating and hospital treatment is usually required to remove the broken tips of spines left in the skin during an encounter. In spite of this deadly protection, hungry triggerfish or triton snails occasionally manage to consume crown-of-thorns sea stars, although usually only as a last resort.

Fishes also arm themselves with protective spikes, warning of their sharp fin spines, but surgeonfishes, and the related unicornfish, have razor sharp scalpels at the base of their tails that are normally folded flat but can be raised in threat if a predator ventures too close. Other small fishes are equipped with strong spines along the back and on the belly that can be locked upright if they are swallowed and do damage to a predator's gut.

Predators often use camouflage colours to conceal themselves from potential prey; but the converse can also be true because some harmless invertebrates and fishes use camouflage patterns to blend in with their normal habitat and escape the attention of predators. Triggerfish and butterflyfish are two groups that use bright colours to warn would-be predators that they make uncomfortable fare. Seahorses and pipefishes are excellent background mimics and render themselves almost invisible against the plants or encrusting animals they live among. Other fishes use disruptive colouration to confuse predators — striking patterns that break up the body's outline, hide the eye and direct a predator's attack toward non-vital body parts, such as rear fins. Small colourful butterflyfish use bright colours as a warning but are also fine exponents of the art of confusing colouration.

Many holothurians (also known as sea cucumbers or bêche-de-mer) are able to extrude a mass of very sticky toxic tentacles, called cuvierian tubules, from the anus if they are disturbed. These are designed to deter would-be predators — a fish suddenly covered in dozens of nasty-tasting tentacles quickly rethinks its priorities.

Leopard sea cucumber *Bohadschia argus* displaying toxic cuvierian tubes used for defence.

Camouflage colours and patterns help many reef animals blend in with their habitat's background. Camouflage can conceal predators from their prey, right up to the critical moment of attack, but it can also help to protect prey from predators. In the case of this ghostpipefish, its camouflage probably serves both these purposes.

Above: Ornate ghostpipefish *Solenostomus paradoxus*.

Opposite: Toxic blue and yellow painted dorid nudibranch *Chromodoris elizabethina*.

Pufferfish, the fabled fugu of Japanese cuisine, store a deadly poison in their tissues. Any predator that tries to eat these slow-swimming fishes quickly dies. Consequently, puffers have become unafraid, almost blasé, because of their unassailable status.

A blackspotted puffer *Arothron nigropunctatus* ranges the reef with enviable impunity.

Young fishes are more vulnerable to predation because of their small size, so have evolved protective strategies to help keep themselves safe. Adult spotted sweetlips are drab-coloured with many dark grey spots, but the juveniles of this species are bright orange with white splotches and large showy fins. To discourage predators, these small fishes swim with a highly exaggerated side-to-side motion — a style that resembles the movements of a toxic flatworm.

Juvenile colour of spotted sweetlip
Plectorhinchus chaetodonoides.

Sharp spines are a popular deterrent on coral reefs, and sea urchins have needle-sharp spines that discourage most predators. Large triggerfish will sometimes brave this forbidding rampart if they are particularly hungry, but most predators seek easier fare. Toxic fin spines are also employed for protection. Butterflyfishes have strong spines that can be locked upright — making them a very prickly and unpalatable mouthful.

Above: Reef sea urchin *Echinothrix calamaris.*

Opposite: Saddle butterflyfish *Chaetodon ephippium.*

CORAL SPAWNING

Although coral colonies can live for at least 1000 years, they need to reproduce themselves in order to spread to other places and contribute their genes to the next generation.

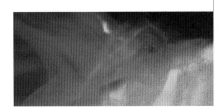

Many corals can reproduce asexually — without the initial union of eggs and sperm. Storms and cyclones smash up fragile coral colonies and scatter still-living fragments over a wide area. Many of these fragments continue to grow and become "daughter" colonies located some distance from "parent" colonies. Many soft corals and sea whips can voluntarily "bud off" parts from the parent colony, they then roll a short distance across the bottom before re-attaching and growing into a new daughter colony. Both the mushroom soft coral *Sarcophyton* and the sea whip *Junceella* are often found in extensive clumps containing lots of "individuals" that all share the same genotype. Other soft corals (such as the small feathery clumps of *Efflatounaria*) reproduce asexually by sending out long "stolons" that attach to the bottom and begin to grow a new daughter colony up to 30 centimetres away from the parent colony.

Stony corals and soft corals also reproduce sexually. Most of them do so in spectacular fashion, with hundreds of species synchronising their spawning over one or two nights during spring. Similar species usually deliberately avoid spawning together, minimising the risk of interspecies fertilisation or hybridisation. Scientists are unsure why corals have chosen this intriguing group spawning strategy, but speculate that it may be a means of totally overwhelming all egg-eaters, both in the plankton and on the reef, and thus improving the chances of survival for the young coral larvae.

Because they cannot move, corals cannot gather together to spawn. Instead, they must have some cue that enables them to release eggs and sperm simultaneously — making it easier for their tiny swimming sperm to find the right egg in the vastness of the open ocean above the reef. Corals rely on the moon as their cue to spawn. During October or November, once the spring water has become warm enough, corals ready their eggs and sperm, which have been developing for months, for spawning. A couple of hours after sunset on the appointed night, usually four or five days after the full moon, most hard and soft corals release their eggs and sperm in an incredible orgy that tints the surface of the sea pink with a mass of accumulated eggs. Some spawning activity may occur a few nights either side of the big night, but most of it happens over a single night. Mushroom corals *Fungia* and boulder corals *Porites* have separate male and female individuals, but most other corals are hermaphrodites that release bundles containing about eight eggs with packets containing thousands of sperm.

After they are released from the mouths of the coral polyps, the bundles of eggs and sperm float to the surface where they break up — and then the fun begins! Sperm stream from their packets and begin the frantic search for an egg of the same species. Most of them get it right, but many become confused and fertilise the wrong egg. As a result of these occasional slip-ups during the reproductive melee of mass spawning, hybrids are common among some groups of coral, especially the *Acropora* genus,

Once an egg is fertilised, it develops into a weak-swimming larvae covered in cilia and is known as a planula. These planulae usually only drift with the plankton for a few days before they swim back down towards the bottom to seek out a reef, where they can settle and begin to grow into a new coral colony. It is thought that many larvae manage to settle back onto the same reef where they were spawned, but it is not clear how the weak-swimming planulae manage this feat after spending several days drifting at the whim of oceanic currents. If they do not find a suitable place to call their own, some planulae can delay settlement for up to a month or more and may eventually settle far from their reef of origin. Like all other encrusting animals, a coral larva cannot change its mind once it has chosen a place to settle and start its growth into a young coral. If it has made a bad choice it is doomed. Most corals die either during the larval stage or shortly after they have settled to the bottom.

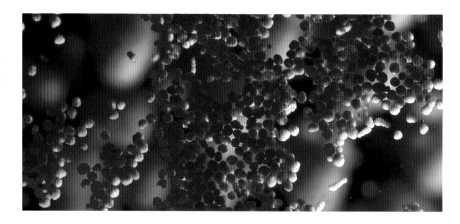

A few hours after sunset, about four days after the full moon in spring, hundreds of species of stony corals and soft corals all spawn together. This renowned mass-spawning event has long puzzled scientists since it seems to encourage hybridisation among similar coral species. It is thought that overwhelming predators of plankton eggs with a "sheer weight of numbers" strategy is more important than the risk of fertilising the wrong egg.

Bright red bundles of eggs and sperm spawned by an *Acropora* coral.

Hermaphroditic stony corals release reproductive bundles that contain groups of eggs and packets of sperm. These bundles float to the surface, where the eggs and sperm separate and fertilisation occurs. Other corals have separate male and female colonies that release eggs or sperm into the water, where fertilisation takes place. In Porites boulder corals, male colonies release sperm that enter a female polyp to fertilise the eggs. The eggs are then brooded in the female polyp until the developing planula larva is ready to swim off and find a suitable place to settle.

Above, left to right: A cloud of sperm is released from a mushroom coral *Fungia* sp.; Pink bundles of eggs and sperm about to be released from plate coral *Acropora hyacinthus*.

INVERTEBRATE SPAWNING

Unlike corals, most invertebrates are not permanently attached to the bottom, but many still have little or no mobility. Such invertebrates (giant clams for example) have trouble getting together to spawn.

Immobile invertebrate species have developed methods of synchronising their spawning so that eggs and sperm have a good chance of consummation. One feather star species that has been studied in Japan has carried this synchronicity to extremes — the entire population spawns over a period of a few hours during a single day in October!

Another method for ensuring the eggs of immobile and segregated species are fertilised is to use chemical cues. A lot of marine animals are extremely sensitive to chemical signals released by other members of the same species during spawning. These chemicals spread through the water, setting off neighbouring individuals in a chain reaction that soon has all the population spawning. Giant clams, holothurians, sea stars, feather stars and sea urchins all use a mix of environmental and chemical cues to ensure that they all spawn at the same time. At late afternoon or early morning, they can often be seen releasing a cloud of eggs or sperm from their reproductive pores.

Invertebrates such as nudibranchs and flatworms do have some mobility, but they still cannot crawl long distances to participate in group spawning. The reproductive strategy of these invertebrates is to adopt a hermaphroditic lifestyle. Each nudibranch is simultaneously both a male and a female, thus ensuring consummation whenever two individuals meet. When they do meet, it is always spawning season! They immediately come together, right sides touching, and each inserts a male organ into the female opening of the other. Depending on the species, they may stay joined for a few minutes or for many hours before separating. Each individual then lays a colourful, frilly, spiral egg mass containing thousands or hundreds of thousands of eggs. Some of the sponge toxins that protect the nudibranch from predation are incorporated into the egg mass, protecting it from hungry, predatory fishes. The eggs hatch as tiny shelled "veliger" larvae, which are able to swim and feed in the plankton and will only settle to the bottom and metamorphose into young nudibranchs if they detect sponge species, which constitute their normal food.

Nudibranchs are fast-growing and have short life spans. Those that feed on sponges (like the painted dorids and Spanish dancer) have the longest life (about a year), but some species are able to complete their entire life cycle in a frantic 25 days!

Fast-swimming invertebrates, such as squids and cuttlefishes, often gather in massive groups to spawn. Groups of females usually attach their large eggs to the bottom in clumps, and hovering males fertilise them as the females lay their egg capsules. Like nudibranchs, most squid and cuttlefish live a short, frantic life of about one year and die shortly after spawning. Unlike many other invertebrates, squid eggs hatch as miniature versions of adults, rather than as a planktonic larval form.

At spawning time, groups of squid gather together to court and lay their eggs. Females lay clusters of rubbery white egg capsules, containing a number of eggs, which are attached to the bottom under coral ledges. Males then approach and fertilise the eggs.

Courting bigfin reef squid *Sepioteuthis lessoniana*.

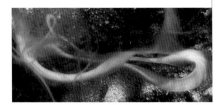

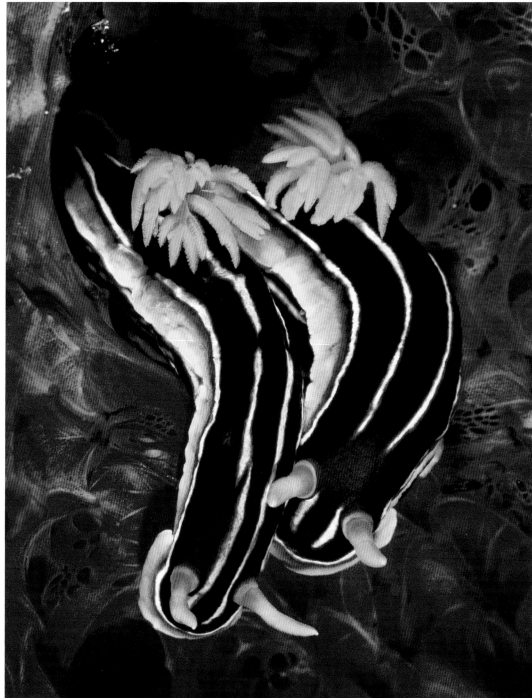

Slow-moving or attached reef animals experience difficulties coming together to reproduce and must find ways to synchronise their spawning activities. Like corals, some take their cues from the moon and the tides. Holothurians also release chemical triggers when they spawn, which can be detected by nearby animals to stimulate spawning. Slow-crawling nudibranchs are usually rare and have a different strategy — each nudibranch is a hermaphrodite (both male and female) and any pair that meet can effectively reproduce.

Above, left to right: A male sea cucumber (or holothurian) *Thelenota ananas* spawning; A pair of Kuiter's painted dorid nudibranchs *Chromodoris kuiteri.*

Crinoids have no body cavity to contain their gonads, so eggs and sperm develop in modified pinnules near the base of each arm. Echinoderms, such as crinoids, sea urchins and sea stars, generally use moon cues and chemical signals to synchronise their spawning.

A spawning feather star or crinoid.

FISH SPAWNING

Many species of reef fish gather in large spawning schools and swim long distances across familiar "reef highways" to reach ideal spawning sites. Fish coordinate these gatherings at times when water conditions are just right to sweep the fertilised eggs away from the reef and its voracious wall of mouths.

The dusky surgeonfish (*Acanthurus nigrofuscus*) gathers in dense schools around projecting spurs on the reef front many times during the spring and summer spawning season. Thousands of these fish congregate right on the turn of the tide, rising and falling in unison, as they prepare themselves for a spawning frenzy. After a long build up of excitement, a few groups of 5–10 fish will suddenly rush up from the main school and release bursts of eggs and sperm before diving back into the shelter of the seething school. The intensity quickly builds, and soon dozens of groups are rushing up to spawn — the water above the school turning thick and milky in a cloud of eggs and sperm. Each fish probably spawns a number of times with many different partners during these mass spawns. The ebbing tide draws the eggs away from a host of expectant planktivores, which dare not follow beyond the protective shelter of the reef.

For other fish species, spawning is a more controlled affair. Many wrasses have a rigid territory and seldom stray outside its borders. A territory is usually controlled by a large male, which has a harem of several, differently coloured females that he courts each day with a distinctive and colourful display. He usually pairs up with each female several times a day, spawning in the early morning or late afternoon by rushing up a metre or so into the open water, releasing a small white puff of gametes, then rushing back down to the shelter of the reef. If a territorial male dies, the largest of his females immediately changes her behaviour to that of a male. Within a week or two, she will have changed sex and colour to become a fully functional male.

Many parrotfishes are also sex changers. Small adults are all females (having the initial colour phase), which change sex and colour to become large territorial males (in the terminal colour phase) as they become older. Some species have developed surprising twists to this story. Small females will sometimes change sex to become males, but will not change to the terminal colour phase. These "initial phase" males, as they are called, sneak around in large males' territories passing themselves off as females — even pretending to spawn with a large terminal phase male if courted! These sneaky, "cross-dressing" males develop very large testes full of sperm and when the big male spawns with one of his females they rush in as the eggs and sperm are released and swamp the eggs with ten times as much sperm from their own much larger testes. Once the terminal phase male realises what is going on, he attacks the initial phase male and chases him away. When initial phase males become too well known, they must give up the pretence and change to terminal phase males that fight for their own females.

Anemonefishes have a different type of lifestyle. Born as males, they change sex to females as they become older, but maintain the same colour. Because they are confined to a single small anemone and brood their eggs in a nest, it is advantageous for the female to be larger than the male — a larger female can produce about ten times as many eggs as one the size of the smaller male. Because of the limited space, the adult pair harass younger fish in the anemone to keep them in a permanent state of immaturity. If the large female dies, the male changes sex and takes her place. The largest immature fish then has a growth spurt — quickly maturing to become the new reproductive male.

Many reef fishes spawn in pairs, with the male and female releasing small clouds of sperm and eggs while their reproductive openings are close together. The male usually courts the female repeatedly for some time before she decides to spawn with him. Eggs are fertilised in the water and develop into larvae that spend several weeks drifting in the plankton.

A courting pair of bicolour parrotfish
Cetoscarus bicolor.

Male reef fishes usually employ elaborate courting displays to persuade females to spawn. Such performances often involve spreading their fins as wide as possible, changing their usual patterns and intensifying their colours to make themselves more attractive to potential mates.

Courting display of male fairy basslet *Pseudanthias dispar.*

Wildly disparate male and female colour patterns help ensure there are no reproductive mishaps! Males are usually more spectacularly coloured because it is their duty to attract females. In many fish species, after a year or two, females change sex to become males and also change colour at the same time — this entire process usually only takes a week or two.

Above, top to bottom: Female mirror basslet;
Male mirror basslet *Pseudanthias pleurotaenia.*

Most damselfishes brood their eggs in nests, rather than releasing them into the open water. Male damsels select a suitable nest site, in this case a dead sea whip stalk, and defend it from other males. Several females may lay eggs in his nest and the male then guards them from egg predators until the eggs hatch a week or two later. The eggs hatch into small larvae that swim in the plankton for several more weeks before settling back onto the reef.

A male golden damsel *Amblyglyphidodon aureus* tends his nest.

Cardinalfishes have evolved a strange method for protecting their eggs. As the female releases her large eggs, the male fertilises them and then takes them into his mouth, where they remain until hatching. During this period of incubation, the male cannot feed but the eggs are as secure as they can possibly be.

Male orangelined cardinalfish *Apogon cyanosoma* brooding eggs inside his mouth.

JUVENILE FISH BEHAVIOUR

The vast majority of Great Barrier Reef invertebrates and fishes have a larval stage — spending anything from a few days to many months in the open-water plankton community.

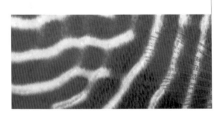

Living among the plankton removes the vulnerable eggs and young larvae from the reef and its wall of plankton-feeding mouths. While allowing animals to colonise reefs far from their original homes, this dispersal stage also presents the developing larvae with a serious problem when it comes time to settle to the bottom and begin adult life — they have to find a reef. Those with a long larval life may end up as far as 1000 kilometres from where they started. Even if they are only carried a few kilometres from where they were spawned, how do weak-swimming larvae find a reef? This is a question that has long puzzled reef biologists; however, some intriguing answers have recently been discovered.

One obvious strategy is to delay settlement if there are no reefs nearby when larvae are ready to find a home. Some species are able to put off settlement for months, regularly descending to the bottom and checking for suitability before returning to the ocean's upper layers and moving on. Scientists have also found that not only can fish larvae swim much faster and more continuously than had previously been thought, they can hear a reef from a distance of some kilometres, determine its direction and swim towards it. It is clear that larvae are not drifting helplessly at the whim of the currents, but can take a much more active role in finding a home reef.

It was long thought that even short-lived larvae would be carried far from their reef of origin and would be scattered over many different reefs; however, new studies have shown that "self-recruitment" (settling on the same reef as they were spawned) is common in many fishes and corals. By putting a chemical marker into the eggs of a large number of females, scientists have shown that nest-brooding damselfishes and free-spawning butterflyfishes achieve about 20% self-recruitment. This means that one in five larvae of these species settle onto the same reef on which they were spawned, and implies that the larvae have some means of staying close to their reef of origin during their plankton life — the mechanisms for how they do this are not yet understood.

Because the majority of larvae end up in places far from where they were spawned, it is important that they have the behavioural flexibility to cope with a variety of different conditions and a variety of different neighbours. Newly settled juvenile fishes are very cautious and can learn very quickly — another interesting feature of Great Barrier Reef fishes. Most of them immediately learn from any new experience, whether good or bad, and remember their lessons

well. After even a single episode, such as a dangerous encounter with a predator that might be unfamiliar to them, they learn to avoid that animal and do not forget the lesson.

Studies show that some larvae do manage to remain in the vicinity of their parent reef, where they know conditions will be suitable for them. Others set out to find new territories. It is part of the nature of reef animals to seek out distant reefs where some chance event like a cyclone or coral bleaching episode may have left lots of space for them to live, grow and multiply. This constant migration to distant territories, where they may be genetically isolated from others of their species, has led to the great diversity of the coral reef ecosystem.

Young reef fishes often look completely different from adults and display different behaviours as well. The juvenile carpet wrasse (also known as the rockmover wrasse) holds its fins outspread and its body curved as it drifts around near the bottom, resembling a piece of seaweed. Young fishes have a very good memory and experience a fast leaning curve. One example is all they need to lock in an important survival memory. They also quickly retain a detailed map of their environment, which expands as they venture further afield.

Above: Juvenile carpet wrasse
Novaculichthys taeniourus.

Opposite: Juvenile golden damsel
Amblyglyphidodon aureus.

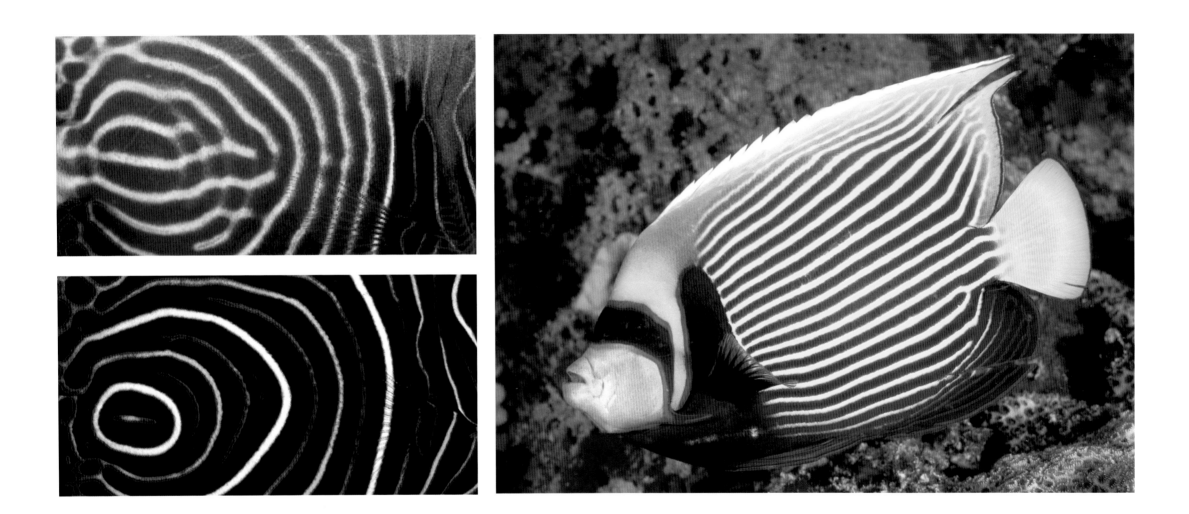

During different stages of growth, many reef fishes display three or more different colour patterns. Newly settled juveniles may have a different colour pattern to immature fish. Adult females then take on another colour pattern, and males may have yet another colour phase. On top of this, adults can often change their colour dramatically to suit their mood, with different display, courting, hunting and resting colours.

Clockwise from top left: The markings of an immature emperor angelfish *Pomacanthus imperator*; Adult emperor angelfish; Juvenile emperor angelfish have more muted bullseye colouration.

LIVING TOGETHER — SYMBIOSIS

The Great Barrier Reef is unique in having such a dense concentration of animals and plants. With so many different species and individuals living so close together, competition for food and space is intense. This has forced coral reef organisms to evolve strategies that minimise competition.

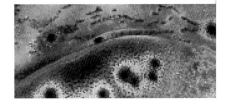

One of the most effective strategies for minimising competition is for a species to participate in a symbiotic relationship with another species. When two species can live together (with some benefit to both parties) they make more effective use of limited resources and reduce competition.

Stony corals, the basic building blocks of coral reefs, are totally dependent on their symbiotic relationship with the tiny zooxanthellae algae that live in their tissues. Many other reef organisms (including soft corals, reef sponges, ascidians and clams) also rely on zooxanthellae for the majority of their energy needs. Evidence exists that all reef-building organisms from the past had similar zooxanthellae and that all ancient reefs were the result of this symbiotic relationship. Whether they were the small reefs formed from primitive, sponge-like archaeocyaths in the Cambrian Period more than 500 million years ago, or the large reefs formed from stromatoporid sponges (together with rugose and tabulate corals) that were so abundant 350–450 million years ago, symbiosis almost certainly played a role in their formation. Modern scleractinian corals evolved in the early Triassic Period, after stromatoporids, tabulate and rugose corals were wiped out during the Permian extinction. However, scleractinians did not form reefs for about 20–25 million years after they first appeared. Scientists suspect scleractinians did not have algal symbionts during this early time and thus did not have the capacity to form reefs. Reef-building ability and zooxanthellae symbiosis seem to be inextricably linked.

Another symbiotic relationship is widespread on coral reefs and plays a major role in creating the coral reef ecosystem of the Great Barrier Reef. The most abundant large fish groups found on coral reefs are herbivores — comprising the parrotfish, surgeonfish and rabbitfish families. Over 100 species, ranging in size from 15 centimetres to well over a metre, make up these groups and all of them are dependant on a range of symbiotic bacteria in the gut to enable them to ferment and digest the plant and detrital food they eat. Without these gut bacteria, and without the warm tropical temperatures that encourage the food fermentation so necessary for efficient digestion of plant material, these fishes could not survive. Interestingly, none of these fish groups are found outside the tropics. As well as grazing on algal turf and any organic detritus or small animals that this turf contains, these fish groups also eat the faeces of predatory fishes. Resting schools of predators usually have a group of faecal-eating herbivores patrolling beneath them, fighting over any droppings that fall. There is still plenty of undigested organic material in the faeces of predatory fish and this is all "grist for the mill" for the bacteria that promote digestion in the guts of these herbivores.

One of the most intriguing examples of symbiosis found on coral reefs is the cleaner–host relationship. Several fish and shrimp species have evolved

lifestyles whereby they obtain most of their food by cleaning parasites, fungal growth and dead and damaged tissue from fishes. The common cleanerfish *Labroides dimidiatus* despite being less than 10 centimetres long, will venture into the mouths of large predatory fishes to pick food fragments from their teeth, secure in the knowledge that it is part of a sacred service industry and free from harm.

Cleaners usually have distinctive, contrasting colour patterns, which are recognised and acknowledged by all other fishes — even fast-swimming pelagic predators. Cleaners also perform a characteristic bobbing dance to help advertise their services. They are territorial and usually set up a cleaning station on some high feature within their home. Other fishes learn the location of these stations and cluster around the cleaners, soliciting their services by posing with fins outspread and mouths agape. Huge manta rays have been seen arriving at cleaning stations and posing while tiny cleaners swarm over their bodies. The dominant male cleaner and several of his females usually attend to each "client", busily picking over fins and body, around the teeth and even into the delicate and vulnerable gills. They remove parasites, clean up patches of infection and pick away bits of dead skin and damaged scales, contributing to the health of their clients and enjoying a safe and ready supply of food. Studies have shown that even fishes with no parasites or skin disease will seek the attention of cleaners. It seems that cleaning is pleasurable to fishes and they like to indulge themselves even when the cleaner's services are not required. Some fish turn up at a cleaning station many times during a single day!

Several shrimp species also provide cleaning services to reef fishes. These shrimps have distinctive colours and perform characteristic dances to attract clients. It is an amazing sight to see these delicate shrimps fearlessly crawling into the open mouths of moray eels and cleaning the teeth of these voracious predators. A client usually gives a signal before closing its mouth — a warning for the shrimps to vacate the premises.

Another well-known symbiotic relationship exists between anemonefish and their hosts; however, there is some doubt as to whether or not this is a true symbiotic relationship. It is thought that the fish helps keep the anemone clean, but this is the subject of some scientific debate. The fish definitely receives a benefit, living safely among the stinging tentacles and away from predators, which would get badly stung if they ever attempted a raid on the anemonefish in its home. So, how do the anemonefish avoid getting stung? An anemone tentacle, naturally, does not sting other tentacles that it touches, recognising them as part of its own body by a mucous coating on their surface. The anemonefish carefully coats itself with the anemone's mucus, becoming one with the anemone and avoiding any stings from its tentacles.

Reef-building stony corals and common soft corals are all dependent on the symbiotic zooxanthellae algae that live in their tissues and provide more than 70% of these corals' food requirements. The algae enjoy a place to live, access to nutrients and a ready supply of carbon dioxide from the coral animal, while, in turn, the coral receives a ready supply of food and oxygen from the algae.

Above: A shallow water, *Acropora*-dominated stony coral community.

Opposite: *Dendronephthya* soft corals do not have symbiotic algae in their tissues and can live on dark, steep walls

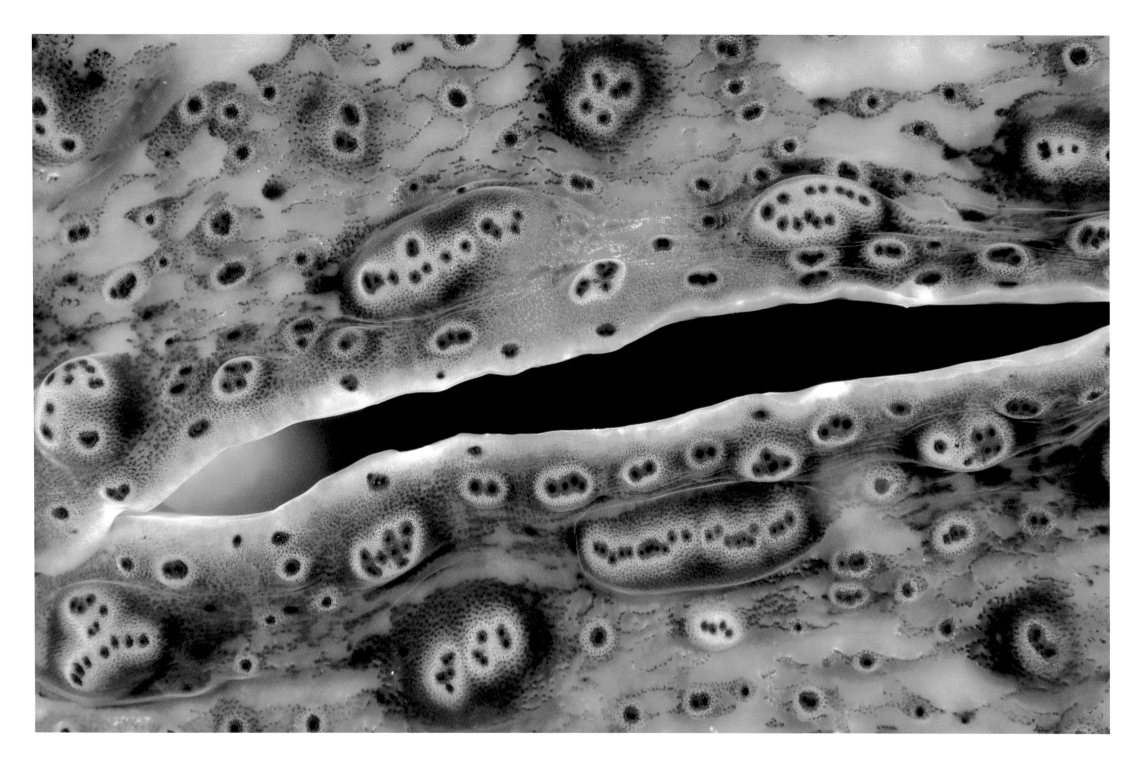

The extra food provided by zooxanthellae also nourishes other reef animals. Soft corals, sponges, anemones, foraminifera and giant clams all have algal symbionts in their tissues. These algae are a dinoflagellate with golden-brown algal pigments designed to absorb the blue light of the underwater world.

An extreme close-up of the mantle of a giant clam *Tridacna gigas*, showing clumps of zooxanthellae in the tissues.

The stinging cells of a large reef anemone can paralyse small fishes, but anemonefishes can live happily nestled among these deadly tentacles by fooling the anemone's triggering mechanism. An anemonefish coats itself in the anemone's mucus, confusing its host which then cannot distinguish the fish from part of its own body. This gives the fish a safe place to live and, in return, the fish keeps the anemone clean.

A pink anemonefish *Amphiprion perideraion* safe in its sanctuary of anemone tentacles.

Several coral reef shrimps and small fishes make a living by cleaning other fishes. These cleaners remove parasites, fungal and bacterial infections, damaged skin and scales, and mucus from the skin, fins, mouth and gills of a client fish. In return for this service, cleaners are off-limits to predators and can safely pick among the razor-sharp teeth of even such feared predators as the moray eel.

A cleaner shrimp *Lysmata amboinensis* attending to a giant moray *Gymnothorax javanicus.*

Cleanerfish set up cleaning stations on elevated, visible parts of a reef or atop large corals. Such locations are visited by many fish and ray species and, in the same way that humans enjoy a pampering manicure or massage, many fishes actively seek out the services of cleaners. Even fish that have no parasites may return to a cleaning station several times a day.

Common cleanerfish *Labroides dimidiatus* cleaning a blue angelfish *Pomacanthus semicirculatus*.

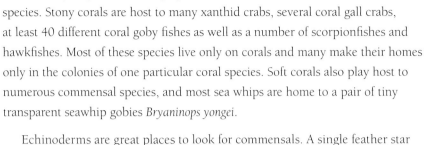

LIVING TOGETHER — COMMENSALISM & MIMICRY

The high animal density on the Great Barrier Reef has led to the evolution of many close relationships. Commensal partnerships are particularly common. In these relationships, one partner receives the advantage of a safe home, while its host animal receives no reciprocal benefit but remains unharmed.

Almost every large reef animal plays host to a number of different commensal species. Stony corals are host to many xanthid crabs, several coral gall crabs, at least 40 different coral goby fishes as well as a number of scorpionfishes and hawkfishes. Most of these species live only on corals and many make their homes only in the colonies of one particular coral species. Soft corals also play host to numerous commensal species, and most sea whips are home to a pair of tiny transparent seawhip gobies *Bryaninops yongei*.

Echinoderms are great places to look for commensals. A single feather star may host two or three species of shrimp, as well as crabs, squat lobsters, tiny cling fishes and bristle worms. Feather stars shelter these animals, but also provide a steady flow of trapped planktonic food — food that becomes a free meal for these hangers-on as it passes down the feather stars' conveyor belts of cilia. It could be argued that some of these associates have crossed the line from commensals to parasites, diverting some of the feather star's energy supply for their own use. A range of beautifully coloured shrimps also live on sea stars, holothurians and sea urchins. Because they are confined to their host, and cannot wander in search of a mate, most of these commensals live in permanent male–female pairs. Eggs take up a lot more space than sperm, so in many cases the female of the pair is larger than the male — often twice his size.

The most bizarre commensals are the pearlfishes that live in the digestive tracts of holothurians and other invertebrates. These small, transparent fishes have long, pointed tails and slip tail-first into the anuses of their hosts. They spend most of their lives inside their hosts and probably feed on host wastes. Many species of pearlfishes live with pearl oysters (hence the name), clams, sea stars, ascidians and holothurians. Some of these fishes are parasitic rather than commensal, feeding on the gills and gonads of their hosts.

Sponges are often hosts for clusters of small synaptid holothurians. Dozens of these tiny, transparent, commensal sea cucumbers (1–10 centimetres long) live on the outer surface of a sponge, using a ring of pinnate mouth arms to feed on organic detritus that collects on the sponge's surface as it sucks water into its internal feeding canal system. Research also suggests that these synaptids actually absorb substances given off by the sponges to supplement their diets.

Mimicry is another basis for many relationships on the Great Barrier Reef. Several animals have evolved the protective strategy of assuming another animal's identity — usually mimicking something that is poisonous or inedible. Not only do mimics evolve colour patterns and shapes that match their chosen hosts, but they also adopt behaviours that make their similarities all the more uncanny. Mimicry is often only employed during the young, vulnerable stages of an animal's life cycle — adults may abandon their mimic shapes, colours and

behaviours. Young round batfish *Platax orbicularis* adopt the shape and colour of a dead leaf — allowing surging waves to wash them around the bottom in imitation of such innocuous vegetation. Young longfin batfish look like a poisonous flatworm, as do the young of barramundi cod and spotted sweetlips. All of these species lose their flatworm colours as they grow larger — their fins reduce in size relative to their bodies and their flatworm style of swimming changes to the normal swimming style of adult fish.

Pufferfishes are deadly poisonous and off limits to predators. A number of fish species have taken advantage of this fact by mimicking the appearance of toxic pufferfish species. Young bluespotted coral trout *Plectropomus laevis* have the same colour pattern as the poisonous blacksaddle toby *Canthigaster valentini*. Although their body shapes are different, coral trout hold their fins erect in a way that makes their body outline more closely resemble the puffer. Other coral trout species (and all other groupers) swim by undulating their bodies and tails, but a young bluespotted coral trout swims by sculling with its transparent pectoral fins, so that it can hold its body rigid in the same manner as a swimming puffer. Once these coral trout reach a length of about 25 centimetres, most of them change to the normal bluespotted colour form and start to swim with normal body and tail undulations. For some unknown reason, a few bluespotted coral trout retain their juvenile colour pattern until they are 60–70 centimetres long. For many years it was thought that these fish, with their white bodies, black saddles and yellow fins, were a separate species called footballer coral trout. The blacksaddle filefish (a small leatherjacket) also mimics the deadly blacksaddle toby, but because the adult leatherjacket is the same size as the puffer, it does not have a separate adult colour pattern. Small leatherjackets often swim with their puffer doppelgängers and their appearance is so similar that a close inspection is necessary to tell them apart.

An Indonesian coral reef octopus, not yet found on the Great Barrier Reef, is the master of mimicry. Wonderpus, as this amazing beast is known, uses its flexible body, eight arms and changeable colour pattern to mimic dozens of different animals. This recently discovered and still undescribed octopus species has been photographed mimicking (among other creatures) flounders, sea anemones, lionfishes, stingrays, cuttlefishes, sea jellies, snake eels, brittle stars, sea snakes, jawfishes and feather stars. It is not known why wonderpus mimics such a wide range of creatures and what advantage the octopus gains from such incredible behaviour.

Opposite: Commensal emperor shrimp *Periclimenes imperator* living on a sea cucumber *Bohadschia paradoxa*.

Commensal shrimps cannot leave their hosts to find a mate, so they usually cohabit in pairs. Females are usually larger than males in order to accommodate a bundle of fertilised eggs, which they carry around with them until the eggs hatch.

Above, left to right: A pair of commensal emperor shrimp *Periclimenes imperator* on a sea cucumber *Thelenota ananas*; Pair of commensal starfish shrimp *Periclimenes soror* on crown-of-thorns sea star *Acanthaster planci*.

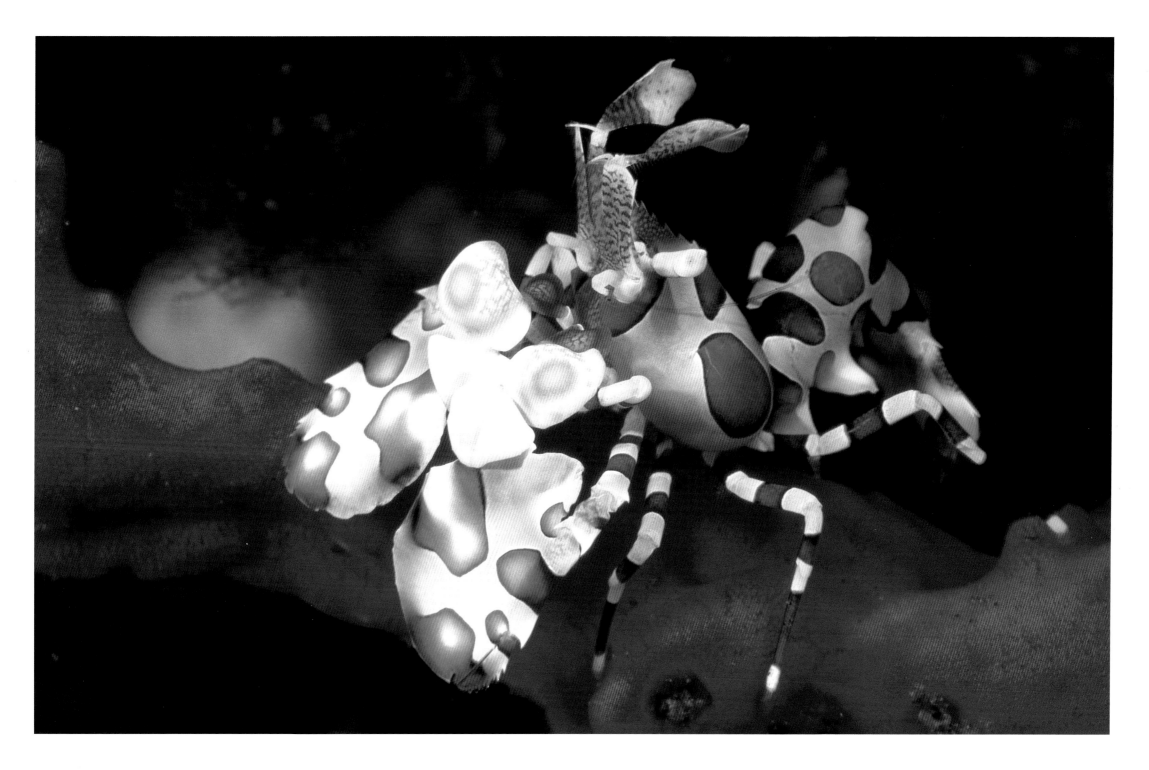

Harlequin shrimps are usually found living in pairs on sponges. Despite their diminutive stature, they are somewhat gruesome predators of sea stars, which they carry with them as a sort of take-away meal — beginning their feast at the tip of the sea star's arms in order to keep the unfortunate sea star alive for as long as possible.

Harlequin shrimp *Hymenocera picta* stationed on its home sponge.

Unusual relationships are a characteristic feature of Great Barrier Reef communities. Crustaceans are particularly fond of commensal relationships with other animals, and most echinoderms have at least one species of shrimp or crab living on them. The anemonefish's unique union with its host anemone is an especially good example of commensal living.

Above: A pair of Coleman's commensal sea urchin shrimps *Periclimenes colemani* on the poisonous fire urchin *Asthenosoma ijimai*.

Opposite: Pink anemonefish *Amphiprion perideraion* hidden within the tentacles of the large anemone *Heteractis magnifica*.

Stony corals, soft corals, gorgonians, sea whips and giant clams are often involved in commensal relationships with gobies and threefins. The host's mucus, along with detritus that collects on the coral surface, nourishes these tiny fishes, which are often found only on a single host species.

Above: Striped threefin *Helcogramma striatum* resting on brain coral *Platygyra* sp.

Opposite: Ghost goby *Pleurosicya* sp. astride a clam mantle *Tridacna derasa*.

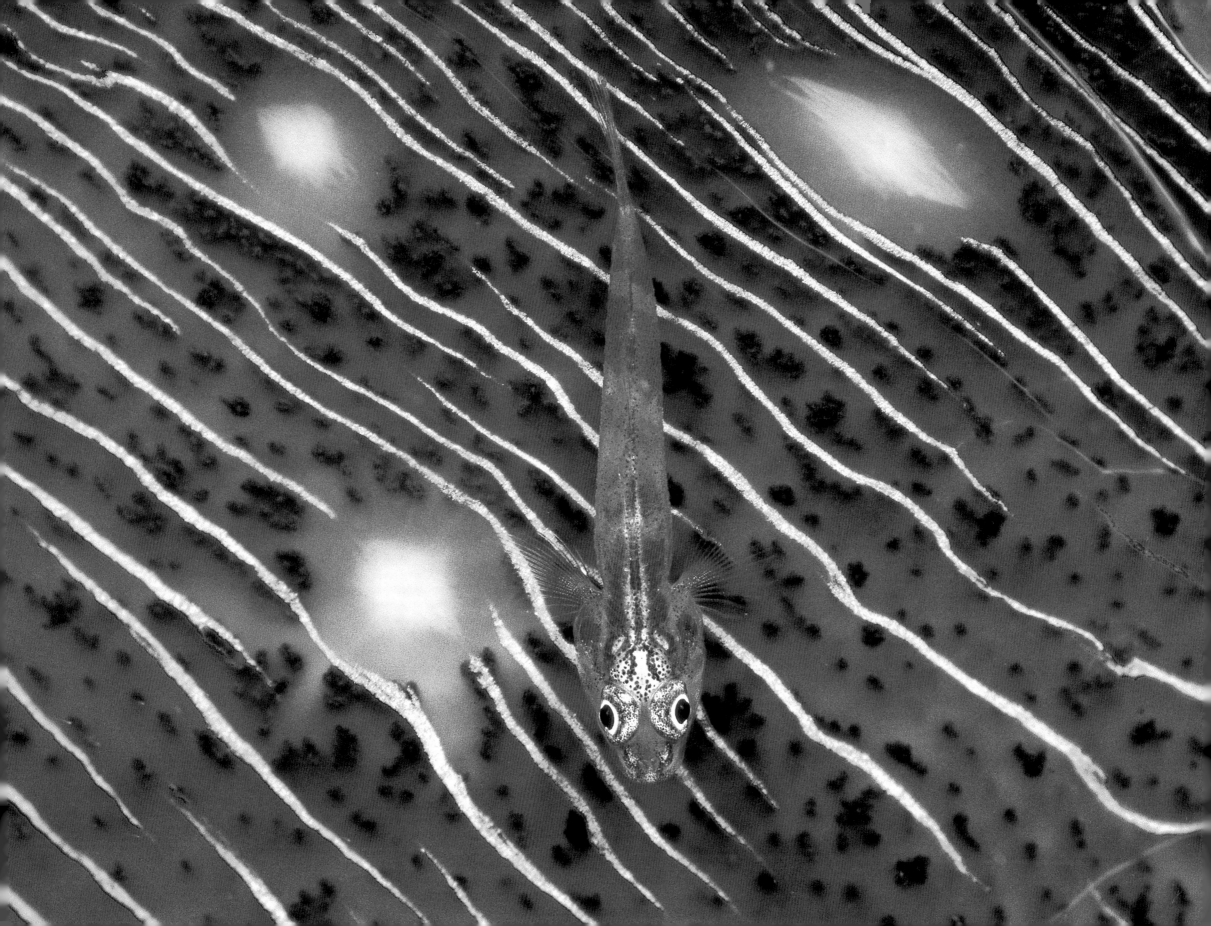

As well as having the ability to rapidly change their colour pattern, octopuses can also manipulate their incredibly flexible bodies into a variety of shapes — two skills that make them exceptional mimics. The remarkable wonderpus, an Indonesian octopus, is an undisputed expert at mimicry, but is yet to be found on the Great Barrier Reef. Related octopus species on the reef exhibit similarly changeable colour patterns.

The reef octopus *Octopus abaculus,* a close relative of wonderpus the mimic octopus, is an agile and intelligent reef predator.

If a predatory fish can evolve a shape, colour pattern and behaviour that mimics an inedible object, they may be overlooked by potential prey until it is too late to escape. These scorpionfishes look like harmless patches of seaweed or dead leaves lying on the bottom.

Above, top to bottom: Weedy scorpionfish *Rhinopias aphanes;* Leaf scorpionfish *Taenianotus triacanthus.*

PATTERN & COLOUR

The coral reef community's endlessly shifting colour palette and bizarre morphology is a constant source of captivation, but why do so many reef animals exhibit such beautiful colours and patterns?

Some patterns are a feature of the physical structure of the animal. The repeating radial pattern of most coral polyps is a function of the basic body structure of cnidarians. All octocorals have a regular pattern of eight pinnate tentacles on each polyp, and most echinoderms have a pentagonal symmetry. The intricate, net-like shape of a gorgonian is actually the most effective design for gleaning plankton from large volumes of water — the form of the animal is an evolutionary consequence of its function. It is perhaps because these forms fit their function so perfectly that we perceive them as beautiful.

Form may follow function, but what function do bright colours serve in the coral realm — especially in animals such as Christmas tree worms, which have no true sense of sight? To consider this question it is necessary to understand how light behaves in the underwater world. Water absorbs light of different colours at different rates. Red is the first colour to disappear (at a depth of around 10 metres). Orange, yellow and green drop out progressively as depth increases, until (at about 50 metres) only blue light remains. To some extent the human eye compensates for this colour loss, and although divers can discern traces of red in deep water, a natural light photograph tells the real story — revealing only shades of blue. The only way to bring out the true colours of reef animals is to introduce artificial light (either with a torch or an electronic flash) and replace the filtered red, orange, yellow and green colours. Most mobile coral reef predators, such as fishes, cuttlefishes, octopuses and squids, have good colour vision, but because they have evolved in a world with very limited red light their view of the world is completely different from ours. Many fishes can see ultraviolet light, which is invisible to our eyes, and it may be that they see various shades of blue as differently as we see red and yellow. Although scientists have some idea of what wavelengths of light fishes' eyes can detect, it is almost impossible for us to visualise how they see their world.

Although a few fishes can make noises, and most can hear low-frequency sounds, reef fishes mostly communicate using colour signals. The colour of most fishes is not fixed, but is constantly changing depending on their age, sex and mood. The different colours and patterns adopted by an individual fish let other reef fishes know whether it is feeling aggressive, subservient, hungry, nervous or ready to mate (as well as many other details). Slight differences in colour patterns let fishes recognise each other as individuals, so that they not

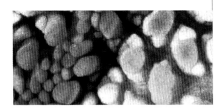

only know, for example, that this is a cleanerfish, but that this is the particular cleanerfish that lives next to the big boulder coral colony and does great work on goatfishes. All the myriad colours and patterns we see and marvel at are actually part of the constant chatter of reef fishes among themselves.

Colours and patterns of animals that cannot see have probably developed in response to evolutionary pressure from those that can. A brightly coloured nudibranch is advertising to keen-eyed fishes that it is poisonous. Over many generations predatory fishes ate fewer brightly coloured animals, until eventually, the glorious warning colours we so admire became a commonly understood warning signal.

Amazing patterns are often a consequence of their function. These soft corals need to spread a wide feeding net from their eight tentacles — the fern-like pattern, which is so appealing to the human eye, is the most efficient way to do this.

Fern-like feeding tentacles of the soft coral *Clavularia* sp.

Cuttlefishes are able to change colour constantly due to their colour cells (or chromatophores) being quickly opened or closed by nerve signals. Multiple waves of colour can pass quickly over their bodies, enabling them to flush red or bleach completely white within a split second.

Close-up of the eye of the broadclub cuttlefish *Sepia latimanus*.

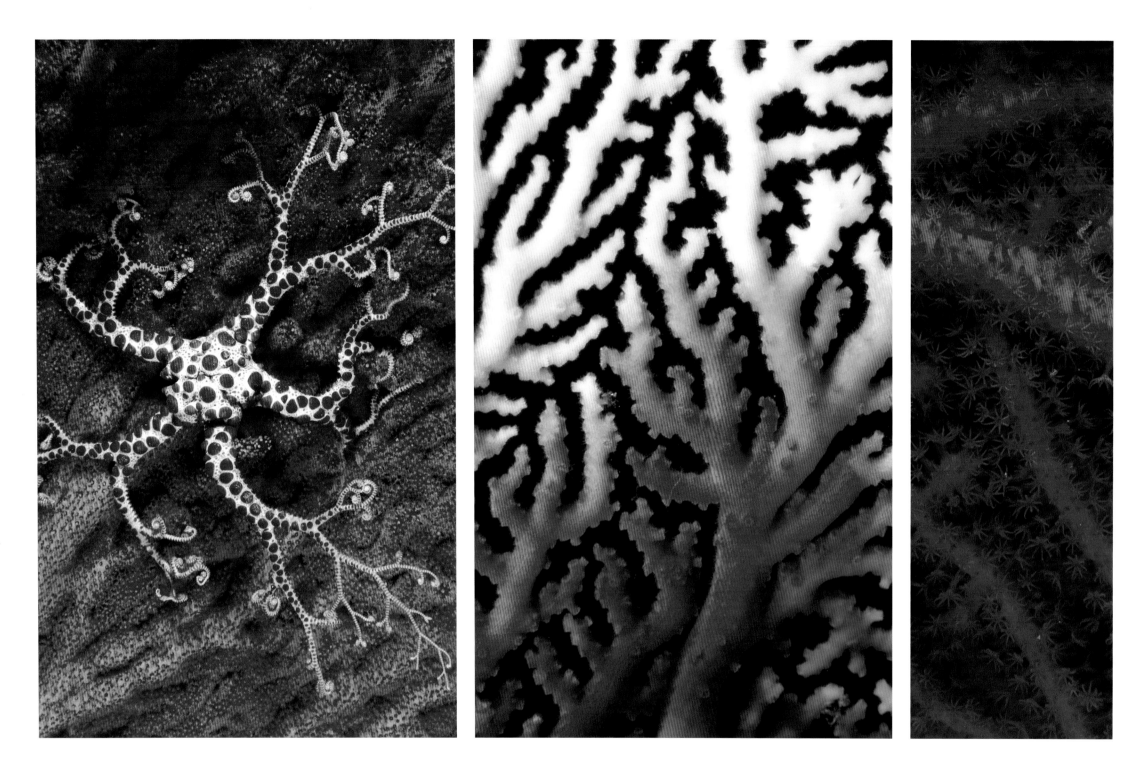

Fan-shaped gorgonians and lace corals provide an endlessly fascinating kaleidoscope of patterns to entrance divers and underwater photographers. These fractal-like patterns on arms covered in plankton-feeding polyps, are designed to enable the efficient filtering of large volumes of sea water.

Above, left to right: A vivid conical basket star *Astrosierra amblyconus* on a gorgonian fan; Branches of lace coral *Stylaster* sp.; Detail of a gorgonian fan showing the many eight-armed feeding polyps.

Opposite: Close-up of gorgonian fan *Melithaea* sp.

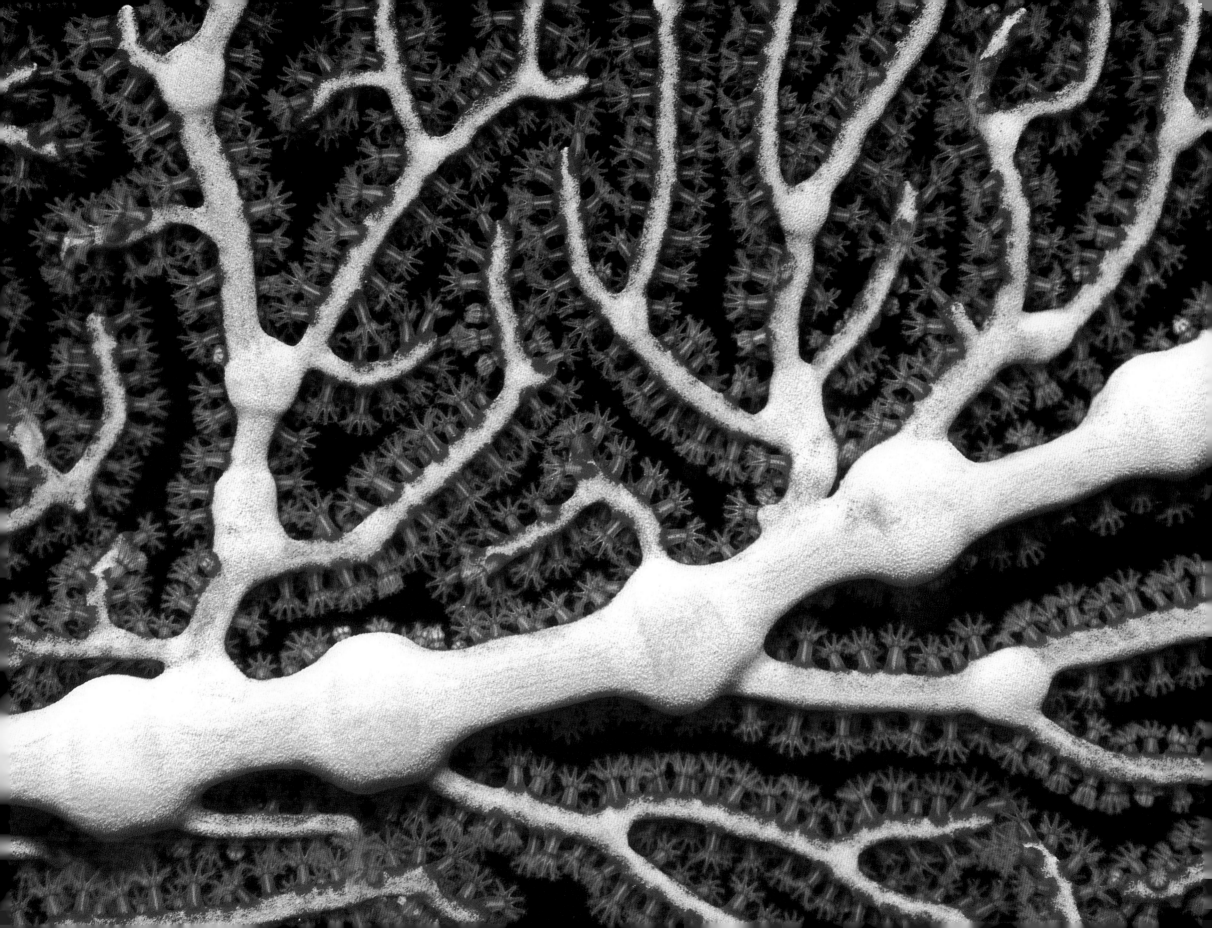

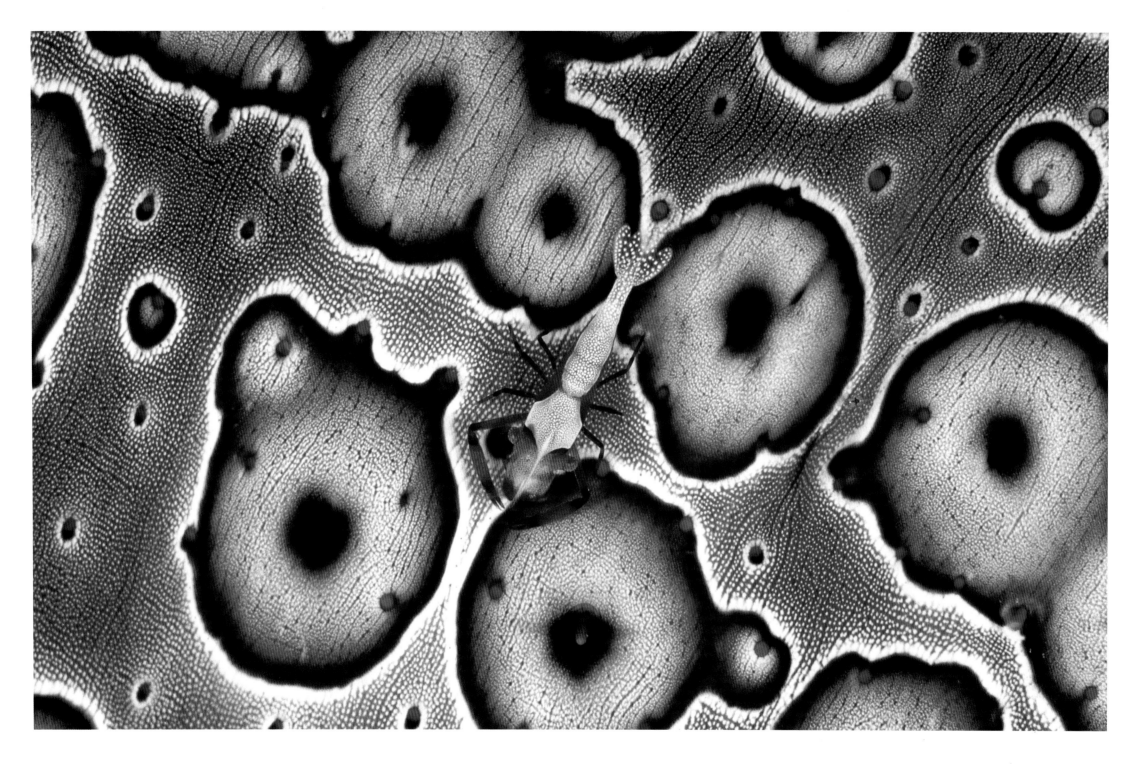

Amazing patterns form an underwater abstract art gallery. The arrangement of tube feet on a sea cucumber, and the protective calcareous plates and tube feet grooves on a sea star, are just two illustrations of the endless geometric pastiche of the Great Barrier Reef.

Above: Commensal emperor shrimp *Periclimenes imperator* on leopard sea cucumber *Bohadschia argus*.

Opposite: Mouth and five tube feet grooves on the underside of the pincushion sea star *Culcita novaeguineae*.

Reef fish colour patterns, when examined in close detail, possess a hypnotic beauty. Although fishes do not have the level of instantaneous control that octopuses and cuttlefishes are capable of, they are still able to vary their colour according to their mood, the time of the day and their stage of life.

Detail of the scale colours of a goatfish
Parupeneus sp.

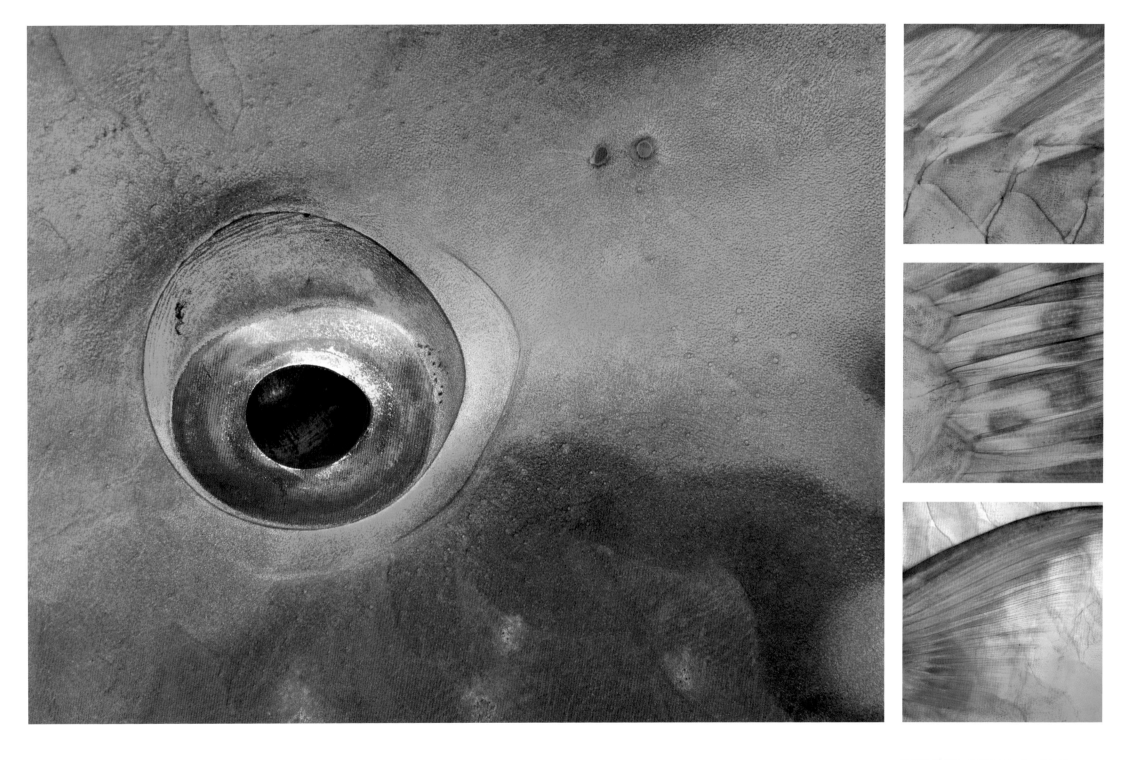

Details of colour patterns surrounding the eye, dorsal fin, tail and pectoral fin of a parrotfish *Scarus* sp.

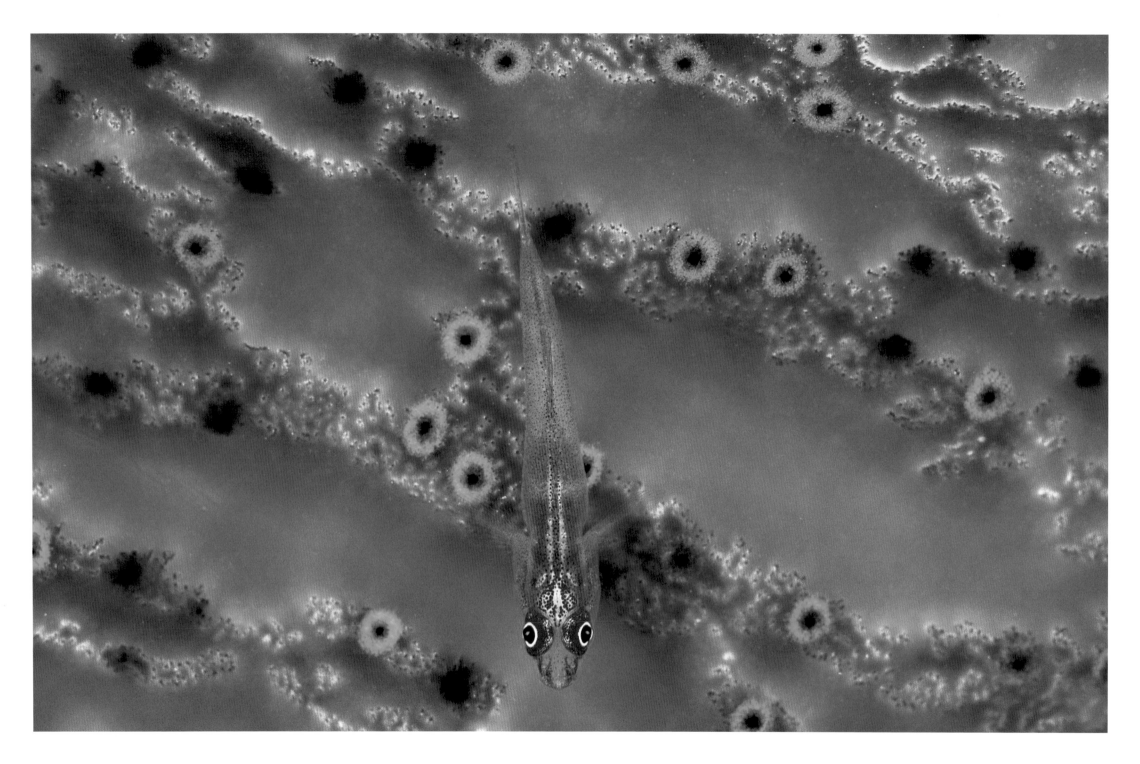

Golden patterns on the giant clam mantle (above) mark the areas where zooxanthellae are farmed within the tissues; however, it is not always this easy to explain the significance of colours seen on the reef. The sensual blue patterns on the Tridacna squamosa *mantle (opposite) serve no obvious function.*

Ghost goby *Pleurosicya* sp. on giant clam mantle
Tridacna gigas

Above, left to right: Inhalant siphon of giant clam *Tridacna squamosa*; Exhalant siphon of giant clam *Tridacna squamosa*.

CHARISMATIC MEGAFAUNA — FISHES

Scientists studying marine animals have coined the playful term "charismatic megafauna" to describe any creature that grows more than a metre long and is harmless to humans. Encounters with these wonderful giants are awe-inspiring indeed, but not something that can be guaranteed on every reef visit. Such creatures are often only seen when specific habitats are visited at the right time of year.

Adult male humphead Maori wrasse may reach over 2 metres in length, but because of their habit of keeping their fins fully spread they appear much bigger. In spite of their immense size, these spectacular fishes are generally very wary and effortlessly keep their distance from divers with lazy beats of their huge pectoral fins. Maori wrasses may become accustomed to divers at regular tourist destinations and associate them with free food handouts. They eventually become tame enough to touch — rewarding visitors with a thrill revered among reef divers. Male humphead Maori wrasse have extensive territories and normally range over an area of many square kilometres. These rare fishes grow slowly, taking about eight years to reach maturity as a female. At fifteen years of age, some females change sex to become males and experience a rapid growth spurt, making males much larger than females of the same age. A large Maori wrasse may be more than 35 years old. They were once sought after as a food fish and could fetch hundreds of dollars if shipped to Asian markets. Fortunately, they are now totally protected on the Great Barrier Reef and in a few decades their numbers should build up again so that they become a more frequent sight, thrilling visitors with their sheer bulk and majesty.

Several species of cod and grouper grow large enough to get the heart pumping on the rare occasions they are encountered. The most well-known fish in this group is the potato rockcod *Epinephelus tukula*, a large cod with an attractive pattern of dark spots on a white background. These imposing fish reach a length of 1–2 metres and are only found on the northern Great Barrier Reef, where they are most often seen in passes between reefs on the outer barrier. About 30 years ago a group of reef explorers started feeding an aggregation of these cod in the pass at the top end of Ribbon #10 Reef near Lizard Island. As word spread, more and more cod (and subsequently more and more visitors) were attracted to this pass. Eventually, the name "Cod Hole" was coined and the site became well known in international diving circles. During its heyday in the 1980s, 15–20 potato rockcod frequented the Cod Hole, milling around divers and demanding a free feed, but numbers have steadily declined since then, possibly due to death of the fish through old age. The largest and most dramatic of the cod species is the Queensland groper *Epinephelus lanceolatus*, a huge fish that reaches a length of 2–3 metres. Queensland gropers are not often seen; when they are, their intimidating presence and monstrous gape make it hard not to imagine them swallowing a human whole! Scientists know very little about the lifestyle of Queensland gropers, except that they are found in estuaries when they are young and probably change sex. Adults are solitary wanderers and are now protected.

One of the largest and most charismatic of all marine megafauna is the manta ray — phantom wanderer of the tropical seas. Spanning 4 metres, these huge, graceful rays occasionally inhabit most reefs throughout the Great Barrier Reef World Heritage Area, although there are a few places, such as North Reef in the Capricorn–Bunker Group, where they are more likely to be seen. Mantas are harmless plankton feeders and their preferred haunts are in places where currents concentrate their planktonic food. Often, mantas are found in groups, following each other along current lines. A manta sighting is the highlight of any visit to the reef, but one that few people are lucky enough to experience.

The whale shark is the largest shark in the world and the undisputed president of the megafauna club. Like the manta ray it is a harmless plankton feeder that is occasionally seen on the Great Barrier Reef during summer. A large whale shark may be over 10 metres long, and with a unique pattern of white stripes and spots on a brown background these nomadic leviathans are unmistakable. Whale sharks may be seen on the front of the outer barrier line of reefs, but are most commonly seen during autumn off the Ningaloo barrier reef in north-west Western Australia.

Much of the lifestyle of whale sharks is still a mystery, although scientists are now attempting to reveal some of their secrets by fitting satellite tracking devices and small video cameras to Western Australian whale sharks. Early tracking attempts struck a snag when the sharks immediately dived to the bottom, scraping off both tag and camera unit, but useful information is now starting to be discovered. For some unknown reason, these sharks make regular trips to the surface when they are feeding and it is during these short excursions that we see them. They make long migrations to rich feeding areas but no details of these migrations are known, nor is there any information available on how fast they grow or how long they live. Most people experience an adrenalin rush when they first sight this magnificent shark, and swimming with one of these amazing, enigmatic creatures rates as one of the most exhilarating experiences for any visitor to the Great Barrier Reef.

Enormous manta rays are gentle giants that feed on plankton animals and small fishes. A manta ray's food is funnelled into its huge mouth by the strange head lobes that extend forward from each side of its mouth. An encounter with these graceful creatures is the high point of any reef dive.

Resembling bizarre alien jets, a pair of manta rays *Manta birostris* soar across the reef floor.

The whale shark is the world's largest fish and roams the tropical oceans of the world, but scientists know surprisingly little about its lifestyle. These magnificent leviathans are rarely encountered, but provide a great thrill for any divers fortunate enough to chance upon them. Groups of whale sharks have been seen during autumn off Ningaloo Reef near North-West Cape in Western Australia, but similar aggregations have not been sighted in the Great Barrier Reef region.

One of the Great Barrier Reef's most enigmatic inhabitants is the whale shark *Rhincodon typus.*

At the famous Cod Hole, on the northern outer barrier reef, a group of more than 20 large potato rockcod have been fed by divers and boaties for the past 30 years. Swimming with such massive, confident fish has energised the dives of thousands of visitors over the years. Natural mortality, however, has taken its toll — there are now only a handful of these impressive beasts remaining.

The charismatic potato rockcod
Epinephelus tukula.

A large male humphead Maori wrasse may be over 2 metres long and weigh almost 200 kilograms. Despite their colossal size these fish are normally very wary of divers, although some habitually visit popular dive sites where divers offer food. At these sites, resident wrasse can sometimes be approached closely enough to touch.

Opposite: A diver swims with a huge humphead Maori wrasse.

Above: Characteristic tattoo-like markings adorn the head and brow of the humphead Maori wrasse *Cheilinus undulatus*.

TURTLES

The first turtles were shelled contemporaries of the earliest dinosaurs and have remained virtually unchanged for several hundred million years. These archaic, armoured reptiles are well represented on the Great Barrier Reef, with six different species spending time in the World Heritage Area.

Turtles are frequently encountered on dives throughout the Great Barrier Reef Marine Park. Six of the world's seven known species of marine turtle — green, hawksbill, olive ridley, flatback, leatherback and loggerhead turtles — grace the waters of the Great Barrier Reef, with the green turtle and the hawksbill turtle being the most common species. An adult green turtle has a carapace length of about a metre, while hawksbills are slightly smaller at between 70–80 centimetres long. Loggerhead turtles are roughly the same length as green turtles, but can be distinguished by their bulkier frame and much larger heads. Flatbacks, too, are similar in size to green turtles, but have slightly flatter shells. The smallest turtle species is the olive ridley — a rare, inshore species that has more carapace scales than other turtles. The largest is the leatherback turtle — an oceanic nomad with a carapace length of more than 1.5 metres.

All turtle species are incredibly slow-growing and do not reach sexual maturity until they are 30–50 years old. Mature females only breed every 2–7 years. When they are ready to breed, they return to the same beaches or cays where they were hatched decades earlier. This amazing migratory feat sometimes requires a swim of more than 1000 kilometres — how turtles unerringly navigate back to beaches they have not visited for 30–50 years remains a mystery! Males gather near breeding sites early in the season and mate with females as they arrive, using special flipper claws to grip the female's carapace. There is intense competition among males — they often try to dislodge mating couples, tearing at the hind flippers of attached males with their beaks.

Females spend the summer near their breeding beaches, coming ashore every two weeks to nest, until they have laid approximately six clutches of eggs. After crawling laboriously up the beach at night, a female uses her paddle-like flippers to scrape out a shallow nesting hole above the high-tide mark. Here, she lays 50–150 ping-pong-ball-sized eggs before filling the hole and returning to the sea. Six or seven weeks later, the baby turtles hatch and dig their way out of the nest, usually at night to avoid predators in their perilous dash for the ocean. The tiny hatchlings that do make it into the water will swim constantly for three days, heading straight out to sea and not even stopping to eat! It is a swim for survival — the hatchlings must run the gauntlet of predatory fishes and sharks, which gather around nesting beaches and cays, anticipating an easy feast. Nothing is known about the early offshore life of baby turtles, but it is thought they drift on the surface far out to sea, feeding on sea jellies and other large planktonic animals. Once they have grown to 25–30 centimetres long, the young turtles move inshore and begin feeding with adults.

Raine Island, a small coral cay on the northern outer barrier reef, is the most famous of the turtle rookeries. Each year, tens of thousands of green turtles gather off the island to breed. Numbers fluctuate, but in some years there may be as many as 14,000 females on the beach in a single night. The turtles that nest here have been isolated so long from those in other parts of the Great Barrier Reef that they are now genetically distinct. In another 10,000 years or more, this population may form a separate species that can no longer breed with green turtles from other regions.

Marine turtles fly through the water by sculling with their front flippers, using their back flippers only for steering. They can swim incredibly fast when they feel threatened and effortlessly outdistance pursuing divers. Turtles grow slowly, but if unmolested they can live as long as most humans. They are extremely vulnerable to exploitation and mortality from fishing nets and set lines.

Green turtle Chelonia mydas.

Hawksbill turtles are slightly smaller than green turtles and have a narrower, more pointed beak. Unlike the herbivorous green turtle, hawksbill turtles feed on animals — especially sponges. Five important hawksbill rookeries exist on islands in the northern Great Barrier Reef — only the green turtle is more abundant in this region.

Hawksbill turtle *Eretmochelys imbricata.*

The loggerhead is named for the size of its head and beak. Its powerful jaws can crush heavy clam shells and break up solid coral rock to extract prey. Unfortunately, these large turtles are extremely slow-growing and their numbers have been steadily declining due to mortality from nets, trawlers and line fishing. New mandatory "turtle exclusion" devices on trawlers, and improved protection, may have slowed this decline, but it will be years before a definitive picture emerges regarding the loggerhead's status.

Clockwise from left: Loggerhead turtle *Caretta caretta* bathed in light; The distinctive large head and beak of a loggerhead turtle; Loggerhead turtle hatchlings scramble from their nest.

Opposite: A courting pair of loggerhead turtles.

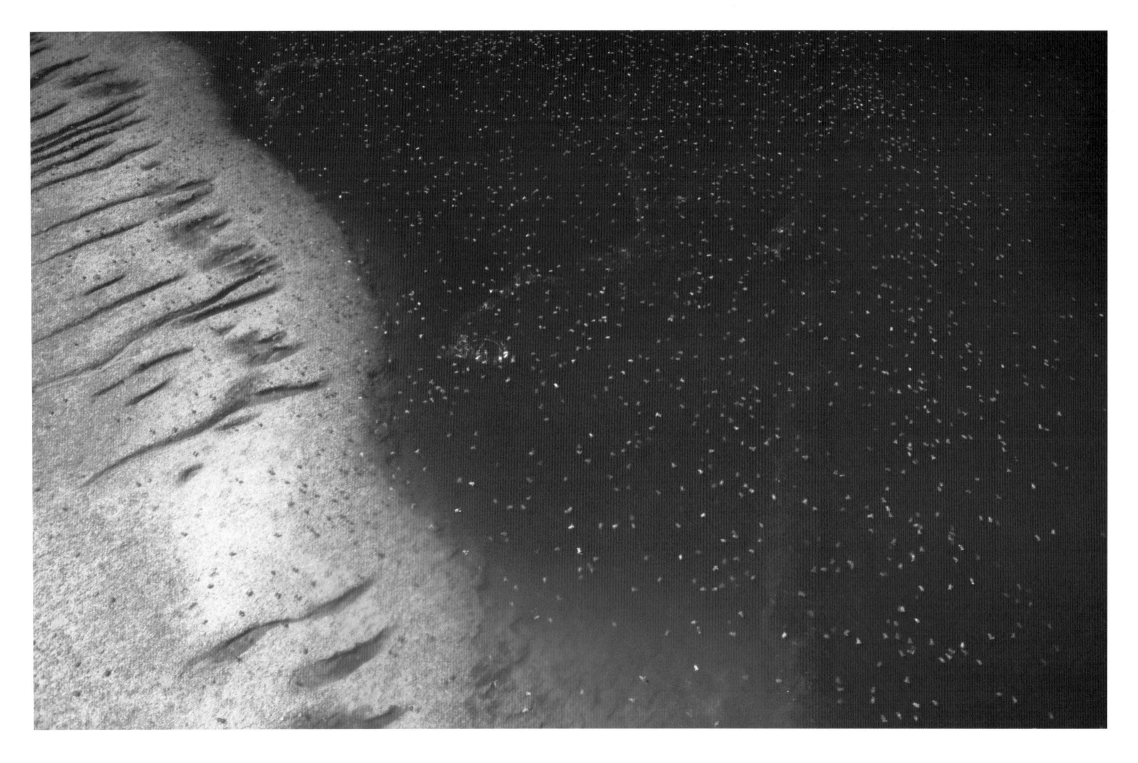

Each year during spring, tens of thousands of green turtles gather around Raine Island. This important cay is the largest green turtle rookery in the world. The turtles mill around in huge groups adjacent to the reef, with each female coming ashore once a fortnight to lay eggs. Tiger sharks also gather around the reef at this time, relishing the "all-you-can-eat" feast of turtles.

An aerial view of the annual breeding aggregation of green turtles *Chelonia mydas* on Raine Island reef.

Green turtles are the most abundant of the six turtle species found on the Great Barrier Reef. Relatively small, blunt heads equipped with strong beaks are suited to their largely herbivorous diet of red algae, seagrasses and the occasional sea jelly. Eighteen major rookeries are found within the Great Barrier Reef area, and a few of these turtles nest on most beaches throughout the reef region.

A green turtle *Chelonia mydas* feeding on a sea jelly.

A pair of mating green turtles *Chelonia mydas.*

Incredibly, turtles return to beach of their birth to mate and nest, sometimes travelling thousands of kilometres from their feeding grounds. Males mate with females when they first arrive off the nesting beaches, and females crawl ashore at two-week intervals, laying a clutch of 50–150 eggs each time. About two months later, the eggs hatch and the hatchlings rush into the water, usually by the light of the moon. Many do not survive the hazardous, exposed journey down the beach to the sea; even fewer escape the waiting oceanic predators.

A green turtle hatchling *Chelonia mydas* emerging from its nest.

SEA MAMMALS

Sea mammals are the ultimate charismatic megafauna! Encounters with our marine mammalian cousins are unique in their ability to inspire us with awe, excitement and a strange sense of empathy.

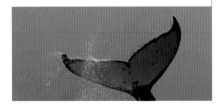

So fascinated are we by our sea-living counterparts in the class Mammalia, that a whole industry has sprung up around whale- and dolphin-watching and thousands of people flock to the Great Barrier Reef's waters every year in the hope of catching a glimpse of these wonderful sea mammals. A total of twenty species of sea mammal have been reported from the Great Barrier Reef World Heritage Area, but only six of these species are common.

Perhaps the most mysterious of these is the dugong (or sea cow), an endangered herbivore that feeds on seagrass beds along the coast of the Great Barrier Reef region. Best estimates suggest that 14,000 dugongs remain in the Great Barrier Reef World Heritage Area, but divers rarely see these distant relatives of the elephant because dugongs usually live in turbid water far from coral reefs. Very occasionally, they are sighted around outer reefs where they sometimes feed on lagoonal seagrass patches. These 3-metre-long, gentle grazers were once widespread throughout the tropical Indian and Pacific Oceans, until hunting and habitat destruction caused local extinction in many areas. Females give birth to a single calf every 3–5 years, with each female only producing about ten young over her lifetime. On top of this, they are slow-growing and long-lived, taking 10–15 years to reach maturity and living as long as most humans — a lifestyle that renders them vulnerable to any unnatural mortality, such as death by boat propeller. Their last stronghold is in northern Australia where they are totally protected.

Ten species of dolphin are found on the Great Barrier Reef, but only three species are regularly sighted by visitors. Close to the coast, and in estuaries and harbours, lives a small, shy dolphin known as the Indo-Pacific humpback dolphin. These distinctive dolphins are usually around 2–2.5 metres long, with a long, pointed beak, a long, low dorsal fin and mottled, pale-grey colouring. They live in small groups and are quite common, although they are rarely seen because they seldom jump and are very shy around boats. Bottlenose dolphins live in small pods throughout the Great Barrier Reef region. Occasionally seen "surfing" the bow waves of passing boats in offshore waters, these large, dark grey dolphins have long beaks, high, hooked dorsal fins and can grow more than 4 metres long. Similarly exuberant are the gregarious spinner dolphins, which are common in offshore barrier reef waters. These attractive, dolphins are smaller than 2 metres long and usually swim in large pods. As their name suggests, they frequently leap from the water and, rather than somersault head over tail, perform an uninhibited aerial display of rapid, upright vertical spins. Like bottlenose dolphins, spinners are enthusiastic bow riders and often launch themselves headfirst from the water as they approach boats or cavort around the bow. Bow-riding dolphins provide endless amusement and often stay with boats for 10–15 minutes before peeling off to go about their business.

Whales are the largest animals found in the Great Barrier Reef World Heritage Area and the most exciting and impressive of all sea mammals. The smallest whales on the reef — dwarf minke whales — grow just 5–8 metres long and are often seen during the winter months. These dark grey-brown, white-patterned whales have narrow, pointed heads and small pointed flippers. Although considered a subspecies of the northern minke whale (rather than a relative of the Antarctic minke found around southern Australia in the winter), they have not yet been given their own scientific name. Dwarf minkes are curious animals that often approach boats and divers, swimming around both at close quarters for extended periods of time. At several places on the northern Great Barrier Reef, dwarf minke whales voluntarily approach anchored or drifting boats and it is possible to swim with them — making the reef one of the few locations in the world where swimming with whales is permitted. Whale–human interaction has been extensively studied and researchers conclude that disturbance to these whales is minimal, providing appropriate guidelines are followed.

Although enormous blue and fin whales are sometimes seen in offshore Great Barrier Reef waters, humpback whales are the largest whales commonly found in the World Heritage Area. At up to 20 metres long, with extremely long, knobby flippers and a bumpy, gherkin-like snout, they are easily distinguished from other whale species that visit the reef. Humpbacks winter in the Great Barrier Reef World Heritage Area, mating and giving birth during their annual stopover in the area's warm, protected waters. Humpbacks do not feed during their time in the Great Barrier Reef; instead, they subsist on thick reserves of fatty blubber stored during their summer glut in Antarctic waters, where they consume tonnes of krill each day. It takes about three months for the humpbacks to make their incredible 6000-kilometre trip from the Antarctic to Australia, and the same for the return journey. An estimated 7000 humpbacks visit this region and the population is increasing by 10% each year.

In some areas, it is now possible to spot many whales in a single day, including mothers resting with their playful young, huge males breaching, fluking and tail-lobbing, and groups of adults moving slowly along their age-old migratory pathways. Males sing during their stay in the tropics, broadcasting their fantastically complex, beautiful songs over long distances. Divers often hear singing whales during winter — the bass notes powerful enough to shake the human body! Prior to modern hunting there were thought to be 10,000 humpbacks in Australia's east coast population. At current rates of increase we should see pre-hunting numbers reached once again within about five years. It will be amazing to see these wonderful creatures regain their former abundance and continue to thrill reef visitors with their awesome size and grace.

Spinner dolphins are the most exuberant of the three dolphin species commonly found in Great Barrier Reef waters. These fast-swimming, small dolphins leap repeatedly from the water, performing impressive spins. Along with the larger bottlenose dolphins, spinners are often seen in offshore waters of the Great Barrier Reef, where they love to bow-ride before boats. The third common species is the Indo-Pacific humpback dolphin, which is generally only seen in coastal waters and estuaries.

A school of spinner dolphins *Stenella longirostris*.

A humpback whale *Megaptera
novaeangliae* tail-lobbing.

Almost 7000 humpback whales spend the winter mating and giving birth in Great Barrier Reef waters before migrating south on the three-month journey to their Antarctic feeding grounds. These whales were hunted to the brink of extinction before they became protected in 1962, but their numbers are now approaching pre-hunting levels and more and more people are enjoying their yearly journey through Australian waters.

A humpback whale breaching.

A female humpback gives birth to a 1.3-tonne calf in the warm, protected waters of the Great Barrier Reef and suckles the calf for one year during their amazing 12,000-kilometre return trip to their summer feeding grounds. Male humpbacks sing elaborate songs and perform tail-lobbing and flipper-slapping displays to attract females during the winter stopover.

Above: A female humpback whale *Megaptera novaeangliae* with calf in shallow reef waters.

Opposite: Humpbacks are the largest whales commonly seen on the reef.

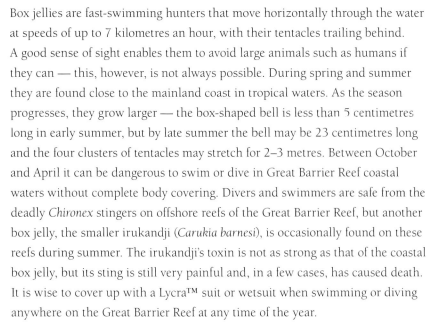

WILD AND DANGEROUS INVERTEBRATES

Among the most deadly of the reef's invertebrate denizens is the box jelly Chironex fleckeri. *This fish-hunting sea jelly has developed a powerful nerve toxin that can kill small fishes within seconds. Unfortunately, it is also capable of killing humans within minutes.*

Box jellies are fast-swimming hunters that move horizontally through the water at speeds of up to 7 kilometres an hour, with their tentacles trailing behind. A good sense of sight enables them to avoid large animals such as humans if they can — this, however, is not always possible. During spring and summer they are found close to the mainland coast in tropical waters. As the season progresses, they grow larger — the box-shaped bell is less than 5 centimetres long in early summer, but by late summer the bell may be 23 centimetres long and the four clusters of tentacles may stretch for 2–3 metres. Between October and April it can be dangerous to swim or dive in Great Barrier Reef coastal waters without complete body covering. Divers and swimmers are safe from the deadly *Chironex* stingers on offshore reefs of the Great Barrier Reef, but another box jelly, the smaller irukandji (*Carukia barnesi*), is occasionally found on these reefs during summer. The irukandji's toxin is not as strong as that of the coastal box jelly, but its sting is still very painful and, in a few cases, has caused death. It is wise to cover up with a Lycra™ suit or wetsuit when swimming or diving anywhere on the Great Barrier Reef at any time of the year.

Box jellies are not the only stingers found in reef waters. The toxin of many sea jellies is so weak that most people are unaffected by the stroke of their tentacles, but a few sea jelly species can deliver painful stings with even the slightest touch. The lion's mane jelly *Cyanea capillata* is one of the largest sea jellies — it can reach a diameter of around a metre and is armed with 10-metre-long tentacles. This huge jelly can deliver a dangerous sting, but is rarely encountered; when it is, its red-brown bell and red-tinged tentacles make it so conspicuous that it is usually easily avoided. The Portuguese man-o-war *Physalia utriculus* is a surface-floating siphonophore sea jelly that is capable of delivering a dangerous, extremely painful sting. Fortunately, man-o-war jellies found in reef waters are usually small, with a float length of only 2–4 centimetres and short tentacles — the sting they inflict is localised and not too dangerous.

Another fish-eating invertebrate that can deliver a fatal sting is the geographic cone shell *Conus geographicus*. It is a strange concept to imagine a seemingly harmless sea shell as a deadly predator, but this cone shell has evolved a potent nerve toxin that is capable of paralysing small fish within a matter of seconds. Geographic cones have a thinner, more bulbous-shaped shell than other cones and are usually mottled brown, pink and white in colour. These attractively patterned cone shells emerge at night and use their acute sense of smell to search for small, sleeping fishes. When a fish is detected, the cone extends its long proboscis, jabs a special long, hollow tooth (shaped like a miniature harpoon) into the fish and injects the poison. The barbed harpoon holds the fish for the few seconds it takes to stop struggling — the prey is then slowly engulfed by the cone's highly distensible mouth and stomach. Cone shells can devour fish more than half their own body length. Cones can also use their toxic harpoons to deter predators and, if handled carelessly, they may inject their poison with no warning. The sting is not usually painful and the first symptoms are numbness or tingling of the fingers and lips. Paralysis and death can result within five hours, but application of pressure bandages (as for snake bite) can delay the onset of symptoms.

The greater blue-ringed octopus *Hapalochlaena lunulata* is another deadly inhabitant of the Great Barrier Reef World Heritage Area. These tiny octopuses are less than 20 centimetres across their outstretched arms, but they can deliver a lethal punch via the venom glands attached to their beak-like jaws. Mottled brown and yellow colouration makes them hard to see when sheltering among bottom growth, but, when threatened, vivid blue rings are flashed as a warning pattern and should definitely be heeded! The bite is not usually painful, but paralysis and death can result in less than an hour. Amazingly, the toxin used by these octopuses is tetrodotoxin, identical to that found in the tissues of pufferfishes. All blue-ringed octopus species are uncommon on the Great Barrier Reef, and with their secretive habits they are rarely seen. Like cone shells, small octopuses should never be handled.

Sharp spines are a risk factor on the Great Barrier Reef and some species of sea urchin are capable of inflicting painful wounds should they be accidentally stepped on or bumped. However, several coral reef urchin species can also inject venom that causes severe pain and irritation. The stinging fire urchin *Asthenosoma ijimai* and the toxic urchin *Toxopneustes pileolus* are colourful Great Barrier Reef urchins that sport either toxic spines or poisonous beak-like pedicillaria. The pain caused by stings from these urchins is intense and the toxic urchin has been responsible for human deaths. Similarly, the sharp spines that cover the body and arms of the crown-of-thorns sea star are also poisonous. Kicking or bumping these spines can cause excruciating pain that lasts for several days and usually requires hospitalisation. A visit to the reef is never completely without risk; however, as long as people are aware of potential dangers, and know what animals to avoid handling, the experience is generally much safer (and so much more enthralling) than driving a car.

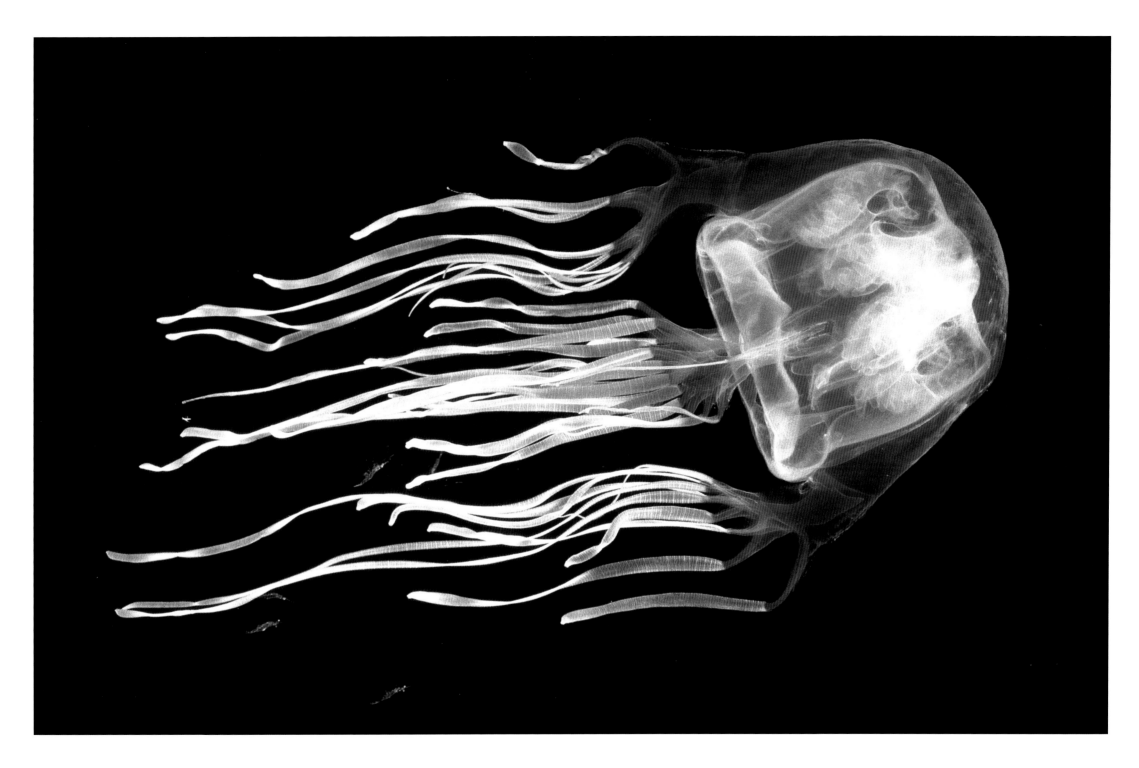

Box jellies are one of the most deadly of the Great Barrier Reef Marine Park's inhabitants. These fast-swimming, fish-hunting sea jellies possess a toxin that can kill humans within minutes — swimming unprotected in coastal waters during spring and summer is not recommended. Small box jellies first appear in October and grow larger throughout summer until March and April, by which time their bells may be over 20 centimetres long and their tentacles may be 2–3 metres long.

One of the reef's silent assassins — the box jelly *Chironex fleckeri*.

The beautiful cone shell may appear benign, but is actually a deadly predator. This slow-crawling sea snail hunts fishes and has evolved a harpoon-like tooth attached to a poison sac that can be jammed into a small fish, ceasing its struggles almost instantaneously. The powerful nerve toxin that works so rapidly on small fishes can also kill humans within hours.

The textile cone shell *Conus textile*, has an extensible proboscis that delivers a poisonous jab to prey and, on rare occasions, to careless humans.

The greater blue-ringed octopus is just as deadly as the box jelly and the cone shell; fortunately, it is rarely encountered. Until they are disturbed these small octopuses appear rather drab, but when annoyed brilliant electric-blue rings flash over their bodies as a warning against their lethal bite. Their potent toxin helps subdue the crabs and shrimps they eat, but is also used as a defence against predators.

Greater blue-ringed octopus *Hapalochlaena lunulata* demonstrating its vivid threat display.

Bumping against sharp sea urchin spines is an uncomfortable experience, made even more painful by the toxicity of several species found on the Great Barrier Reef. Venom glands on the tips of the fire urchin's spines can cause intense, burning pain for fifteen minutes if touched — the effect takes several hours to wear off. The flower-like pedicillaria of the toxic urchin are even more dangerous and have been known to cause death.

Above, left to right: Beautiful stinging spines of the fire urchin *Asthenosoma ijimai*; Close-up of the spines and stinging pedicillaria of the toxic urchin *Toxopneustes pileolus*.

Crown-of-thorns sea stars are formidable predators of stony corals. Aggregations of ten of thousands of these spiny sea stars sometimes occur on reefs and devour most of the coral on a reef within one year. To deter predators, these large sea stars (with a diameter of 30–50 centimetres) are covered in a "crown" of sharp, toxic spines which cause intense pain if bumped. Treatment for wounds caused by these sea stars usually requires hospitalisation.

Above left to right: A crown-of-thorns sea star feeding on a stony coral colony; Close-up of the spines of the crown-of-thorns sea star *Acanthaster planci*, which deliver a toxic, steroid-like chemical compound.

DANGEROUS FISHES

Many reef fish species have venomous spines that are capable of inflicting agonising wounds.

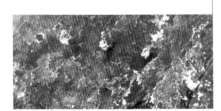

The savage, venomous instruments employed by many reef fish species are designed to protect their bearers against predation, but they are equally effective against careless, soft-fleshed humans. Most of the scorpionfishes have toxic spines on the head and back, and rabbitfishes (or "happy moments" as they are wryly called) have dorsal and anal fin spines that can inflict eye-watering pain. The scalpel-like spines at the base of surgeonfishes' tails are also venomous, as are the paired caudal knives of unicornfishes. Many other fishes are equipped with needle-like dorsal and anal fin spines, which bristle erect whenever these fish feel threatened.

The extravagantly showy lionfish, with its frilly, banner-like fins, has long, grooved fin spines that conceal glands designed to deliver venom into its victim's wounds. Spikes from lionfish spines can cause severe pain, swelling and shock, but have not been known to cause death. The fin spines may be as long as the body of the lionfish and are used for attack as well as defence. Curiously, the lionfish uses these moveable spines to herd small fishes into corners, where they can be gulped down, or stung and immobilised before being eaten. Lionfish also bristle their venomous spines toward any diver who approaches too closely and if this warning is ignored they will lunge forward and drive the spines into the unfortunate intruder.

The ugly overlord of the poisonous fish world is the reef stonefish *Synanceia verrucosa*. As the name implies, stonefish are well camouflaged, resembling stony rubble on the sea floor. Thirteen hollow dorsal fin spines on the back possess enlarged venom glands at the base, but these are used purely for defence. Stonefish are ambush predators, lying unobtrusively on the bottom, vigilantly waiting for unwary prey. When trodden on, they inject extremely potent venom into their victim's puncture wounds. Humans in other parts of the world have died just a few hours after a stonefish sting, but there have been no known deaths in Australia, where an antivenom is available. The pain from a stonefish sting is excruciating and any person stung should immediately seek medical attention.

Fish with poisonous spines are not the only danger to humans on the Great Barrier Reef — a handful of large predators have been implicated in unprovoked attacks on divers and swimmers. Perhaps the most unlikely dangerous fishes are large triggerfishes, such as the titan triggerfish *Balistoides viridescens*.

Triggerfishes have small mouths containing sharp, chisel-like teeth and usually feed on sea urchins, crabs, shellfish and other invertebrates. However, nesting females are vigilant guardians of their eggs and aggressively attack trespassing divers. They can inflict nasty wounds on unprotected body parts and are another good reason to always wear a full wetsuit when diving on the reef.

The ocean-roving great barracuda *Sphyraena barracuda* grows to 2 metres and weighs up to 50 kilograms. With its ragged mouthful of razor-sharp teeth the barracuda is a ferocious predator capable of inflicting maximum damage with a single bite. Great barracuda usually drift slowly through the water, but they can attack at speeds of up to 60 kilometres an hour. When motivated, their strike is lightning fast and so powerful that even a large fish is often torn in two and suspended in a gruesome cloud of flesh particles in the barracuda's vicious wake. Active both day and night, barracuda hunt most aggressively at dawn and dusk. They are inquisitive fish, often following snorkellers and divers for disconcerting lengths of time. They have been known to stake extended claims around tourist pontoons on the Great Barrier Reef.

Barracuda are the cheetahs of the sea. These fast-swimming, pelagic predators can attack extremely quickly, striking at speeds of up to 60 kilometres an hour, and using their razor-sharp teeth to ferociously tear apart other fishes. Despite their size and their menacing appearance, barracudas are harmless to humans on the Great Barrier Reef.

Above: A solitary great barracuda *Sphyraena barracuda* eyes the camera.

Opposite: A diver keeps a respectful distance from a school of blackfin barracuda *Sphyraena qenie.*

The blue tang is a plankton-feeding surgeonfish that lives in the surge zone at the front of exposed outer barrier reefs. Like all surgeonfishes, blue tangs have a pair of incisive scalpels on each side of the base of the tail. These scalpels are used in defence and as weapons in territorial disputes with rival blue tangs and can inflict painful wounds.

Blue tang *Paracanthurus hepatus*.

Rabbitfishes have earned the sarcastic nickname "happy moments" because of the extreme pain dealt out by spikes from their fin spines. When threatened, these gentle herbivores raise their fin spines to advertise the potential consequences of an overly intimate engagement. The spines tangle easily in nets and unwary handling often results in torturous wounds. Soaking the affected area in very hot water somewhat eases the pain.

A pair of goldlined rabbitfish *Siganus lineatus* with fin spines at the ready.

Common lionfish *Pterois volitans*.

Most fish spines are sharp enough to inflict painful wounds, but many of the scorpionfishes and stonefishes also harbour poison glands on their spines that can cause severe pain, shock and illness in humans. Dorsal spines of the well-camouflaged stonefishes contain the most potent of these poisons. Stings from these fishes have occasionally caused death in other countries, but there have been no reported fatalities from stonefishes, lionfishes or other scorpionfishes in Australia.

Above, left to right: Reef stonefish
Synanceia verrucosa; Smallscale scorpionfish
Scorpaenopsis oxycephala.

SHARKS

Sharks inspire a fear far greater than any other reef animal. Many people refuse to swim or dive in Great Barrier Reef waters because they have a phobia of shark attack.

In reality, most sharks on the Great Barrier Reef are harmless to divers and swimmers, so a shark sighting should only add intrigue and excitement to a dive. The three most-abundant large sharks found in the Great Barrier Reef World Heritage Area are the reef sharks — the whitetip reef shark *Triaenodon obesus*, the grey reef shark *Carcharhinus amblyrhynchos* and the blacktip reef shark *Carcharhinus melanopterus*. These three species usually grow to 1.5–2 metres long and are all members of the whaler shark family, which includes most of the world's dangerous sharks. It is not unusual to see one or two reef sharks during a dive on the offshore Great Barrier Reef. All three reef sharks mature at 8–10 years of age and live for 20–25 years. Every two years mature females give birth to a few live young (50–60 centimetres long) and each female only produces 12–15 young in her entire lifetime. Reef sharks are highly territorial and are usually only found close to reefs. Whitetips are unusual among whaler sharks, spending some time resting on the bottom — most of their relatives must swim constantly to keep water flowing over their gills. These common sharks are less dangerous to humans than dogs, but when aggravated they have occasionally bitten divers or fishermen. Territorial grey reef sharks sometimes behave aggressively and make distinctive threat displays towards divers. They have been known to make rapid attacks and deliver sudden warning bites when threatened or provoked.

Several species of large whaler sharks also cruise the Great Barrier Reef waters, but these are uncommon around reefs and are only seen by divers once in every 50–100 dives. Large whaler sharks are usually between 2–3 metres long and are potentially dangerous to humans. They include the beautiful silvertip shark *Carcharhinus albimarginatus*, which is usually seen on steep drop-offs around the front of outer barrier reefs in depths of more than 30 metres. Silvertips are a bronze-grey colour on the back and white underneath with spectacular silver tips and trailing edges on all of their fins. Although they have never been reliably implicated in any human attack, silvertips often behave aggressively towards divers and make close approaches to intruders. Two other large whalers that are occasionally seen around reefs are almost impossible to tell apart underwater. The bull shark *Carcharhinus leucas* and the pigeye shark *Carcharhinus amboinensis* (sometimes known as the black whaler) are both heavy-bodied, dark-coloured sharks with distinctive, sharp-pointed first dorsal fins. Both are potentially hazardous to humans and the bull shark is regarded as one of the four most dangerous sharks in the world — a category also reserved for the tiger, oceanic whitetip and white shark.

Out in the open blue water beyond the Great Barrier Reef, a number of ocean-wandering whaler sharks lurk. The dusky whaler *Carcharhinus obscurus*, the silky shark *Carcharhinus falciformis,* and the oceanic whitetip shark

Carcharhinus longimanus are all large, potentially dangerous sharks that may be encountered in the open ocean within the Great Barrier Reef World Heritage Area. Divers do not usually see these sharks unless they are willing to venture into the bottomless infinity of open water and actively seek them out (by making noises or releasing baits to attract sharks). No attacks by any of these species have been recorded in the Great Barrier Reef region.

Two large hammerhead shark species are also occasionally seen on the Great Barrier Reef. The scalloped hammerhead *Sphyrna lewini* and the great hammerhead *Sphyrna mokarran* are large sharks that may be encountered every 200–500 dives on the reef. Apart from the harmless whale shark, the great hammerhead is the largest shark that lives on the reef. Full-grown great hammerheads may be 5–6 metres long, with very high first dorsal fins and huge upper tail lobes. Unless they are agitated by spearfishing or fish-feeding activity, hammerheads usually take no interest in divers and will swim past and go about their business. However, they can become extremely aggressive when excited by the vibrations of struggling fish or the smell of fish flesh and blood and have bitten a number of divers and snorkellers in the Great Barrier Reef region over the past several decades.

While most sharks eat smaller sharks, fishes, and rays (and do not view humans as a potential meal), tiger sharks routinely eat human-sized prey and are regarded as a genuine threat to divers exploring the reef. Tiger sharks are usually between 3–5 metres long, but the largest reliably measured shark was a massive 6 metres! Fishermen claim to have seen 7-metre-long tigers, and bite marks on whale carcasses suggest they may grow even larger than this, which would make them larger than great hammerheads. However, such estimates are, perhaps, a reflection of the excitement generated by sighting a huge tiger rather than true objectivity. Tiger sharks put on a lot of bulk as they grow and a 5-metre-long tiger shark is an enormous animal. Turtle flesh is relished by tiger sharks, which gather around places such as Raine Island during the turtle-nesting season. The special curvature of a tiger shark's teeth makes short work of carapaces, and a large tiger can tear up and devour a full-grown green turtle with little difficulty — a meal that would probably sustain the shark for weeks. Despite their potential danger and relative abundance, divers rarely encounter tiger sharks (diving around Raine Island during turtle-nesting season is an exception to this rule), and there has never been a confirmed attack on a diver in the Great Barrier Reef region. However, tiger sharks have attacked shipwreck survivors left adrift in the open ocean, and have been implicated in the disappearance of two divers who were accidentally left on the reef by a dive charter boat.

The three most common reef sharks grow to about 2 metres long and pose less danger to humans than do domestic dogs. These territorial sharks have occasionally bitten people who have provoked them, but such a bite is only a warning — not an attempt to eat the trespasser. Small blacktips are often seen hunting in shallow water along the edge of reefs on the incoming tide. Whitetips are the only species of whaler shark that may be observed resting on the bottom.

Above, top to bottom: Blacktip reef shark *Carcharhinus melanopterus*; Whitetip reef shark *Triaenodon obesus*.

GREAT BARRIER REEF | 193

A number of species of large whaler shark are common in the open ocean beyond the outer edge of the Great Barrier Reef. These sharks cruise the endless void of the deep ocean waiting for feeding opportunities. Silky sharks, dusky sharks and oceanic whitetips all live in this habitat, but they never venture onto reefs and are rarely seen unless divers make special efforts to actively seek them out.

Silky shark *Carcharhinus falciformos.*

Due to their sheer size, many species of large whaler sharks are potentially dangerous to humans. The dusky whaler grows to over 3.5 metres long, but is rarely encountered by reef divers, preferring the open ocean beyond the reef. The most dangerous member of the Carcharhinidae family is the bull shark — a large, aggressive whaler shark responsible for more human fatalities than any other shark. Their extreme aggression is the result of elevated testosterone levels — among the highest of any animal in the world! These dangerous sharks are sometimes seen around reefs on the Great Barrier Reef.

Although it prefers warm waters, the dusky whaler Carcharhinus obscurus is rarely encountered by divers on the Great Barrier Reef — living an open-ocean lifestyle beyond the continental shelf.

Tiger sharks are widely distributed on the Great Barrier Reef, from shallow reef flat waters down to the deepest offshore habitats. They are usually more active at night but are sometimes seen swimming around reefs during the day. Tiger sharks are potentially very dangerous to humans but rarely threaten divers on the Great Barrier Reef.

Tiger shark *Galeocerdo cuvier.*

The great hammerhead is one of the largest of the dangerous sharks that reside on the Great Barrier Reef. These piscivorous oddities, with their distinctive "Formula One" shaped head lobes, may grow to a length of 6 metres and have a first dorsal fin over a metre high. Stingrays are this shark's favourite food and scientists surmise that the hammerhead's lobes act like a kind of "stingray detector" as these sharks strafe the reef's shallow sand flats.

Great hammerhead *Sphyrna mokarran* showing its oversized first dorsal fin and perfectly adapted head lobes.

DANGEROUS REPTILES

Giant carnivorous marine reptiles may have become extinct at the end of the Cretaceous period (along with the dinosaurs), but dangerous reptiles are still found throughout the Great Barrier Reef World Heritage Area today.

Most people consider estuarine (or saltwater) crocodiles to be creatures of rivers and estuaries, but these formidable predators are able to live happily in saltwater and have been known to make open ocean voyages of more than a 1000 kilometres. These reptiles have been protected for more than 30 years in Australia, and as their numbers have increased they have reclaimed much of their former territory, including offshore islands, cays and reefs. On the northern Great Barrier Reef, crocodiles are now found on many islands up to 50 kilometres from the coast and they have also been sighted around reefs more than 60 kilometres offshore. The thought of 5-metre-long saltwater crocodiles catching and eating turtles on the outer barrier reef is not a happy one for most reef users, but sightings like this are becoming increasingly frequent. A number of snorkellers and scuba divers have been killed by large crocodiles on offshore Northern Territory coral reefs over the past few years and several non-fatal attacks have also occurred on the northern Great Barrier Reef. While most experienced divers can predict shark behaviour and learn to live with these predatory fishes, the confidence required to share reef waters with large estuarine crocodiles borders on foolhardy.

About twelve species of highly venomous sea snake are also found on the Great Barrier Reef. The most abundant species is the olive sea snake, which has a pale grey body (1–1.5 metres long) and a distinctive brownish head. These snakes probe crevices and holes for small fishes, and their potent venom is designed to instantly paralyse prey that may, in its death struggle, otherwise escape these weak-jawed snakes. Like all reptiles, sea snakes are air-breathing and usually venture to the surface every 20–30 minutes to breathe. On a full tank, sea snakes can stay submerged for at least an hour and dive to depths of more than 60 metres. Flattened paddle-like tails enable them to swim much faster than divers. Olive sea snakes are found occasionally in the inter-reef habitat throughout much of the Great Barrier Reef, but they are only found around reefs towards the southern end of the region. In the Swain and Pompey Groups, some reefs are home to resident sea snakes while others are not. One reef may always support a large population of olive sea snakes, while an adjacent reef will always be snake-free — researchers have been unable to explain the reasons behind this. Olive sea snakes are curious reptiles and will often closely investigate divers, twining around their legs and arms or staring directly into face-masks. This behaviour can be intimidating to the uninitiated, but as long as they are not molested sea snakes soon go about their business and leave divers alone.

Olive sea snake *Aipysurus laevis*.

Relatives of the highly venomous terrestrial elapids, sea snakes have adapted to living in the ocean and their venom is even more deadly than that of their land-based cousins. Flattened paddle-like tails enable easy movement underwater, where they feed on bottom-living fishes which they hunt among the reef's nooks and crannies. The olive sea snake is the most common of the dozen or so species found on the reef.

An olive sea snake *Aipysurus laevis* probing the reef for its prey.

Estuarine crocodiles have been protected in Australia for over 30 years and their numbers have increased tenfold. The world's largest reptile is regaining its former territory and becoming increasingly common on the offshore islands, cays and reefs of the northern Great Barrier Reef. Large crocodiles have even been sighted eating turtles on the outer barrier reef, more than 50 kilometres from shore.

Large estuarine crocodiles *Crocodylus porosus* are capable long-range swimmers and an increasingly common sight on the reef's offshore islands and cays.

While crocodiles will eat birds, mammals and even humans, fish is the mainstay of their diet and they can easily catch enough fishes around coral reefs. In summer, females lay their eggs in nests of raised vegetation and guard them until they hatch. Crocodiles are slow-growing and may live to more than 100 years of age.

The head of a large estuarine crocodile *Crocodylus porosus* crowned in waterweed.

HUMAN IMPACT ON THE REEF

The Great Barrier Reef World Heritage Area is managed as a multi-use marine park, not as a sacrosanct reserve to keep the reef in pristine condition. However, the ideal is to ensure that destructive activities are carried out in a controlled and sustainable manner.

The potential conflict between different user groups (fishing and prawn trawling on the one hand versus tourism and research on the other) has occasionally been the focus of media attention, but overall the reluctant marriage of exploiters and conservationists seems to be working.

Prawn trawling within the Great Barrier Reef World Heritage Area is a major industry, earning close to $100 million annually. Until recently, over 90% of the Great Barrier Reef lagoon (the area between the reefs and the coast) was available to trawlers, but recent closures have reduced that area to about 75%. Trawl fishing is currently tightly managed and only 400 trawlers are permitted to operate in the Great Barrier Reef region. Satellite transponders constantly monitor boats' positions, ensuring operators do not fish in protected zones. While 6000 tonnes of prawns are harvested annually, estimates suggest that around ten times this amount comprises the unwanted (and mostly dead) by-catch discarded by trawlers. Such waste has dramatically altered the marine community over much of the Great Barrier Reef's (trawled) sandy habitat.

Around 500 commercial reef line-fishing boats also operate in the World Heritage Area, removing a total of about 3000 tonnes of fish every year. Over a third of these fish are coral trout, another quarter are redthroat emperor. Studies show that the combined recreational fishing catch is almost equivalent to the commercial catch. There is some concern that this level of fishing is not sustainable. Most of the fishing effort is directed at four or five species, with the coral trout taking the brunt. Given that the average adult coral trout weighs about a kilogram, the combined commercial and recreational catch of this species, following recent catch cutbacks, is about 1.5 million fish annually. If we assume that this is taken equally from the 1000 or so major offshore reefs open to fishing (most commercial line-fishing only occurs on offshore reefs), this equates to approximately 1500 coral trout removed from each reef every year. Counts of adult coral trout have been made on many reefs and it is possible to calculate that there are, on average, about 6000 living on each reef. This calculation suggests that fishermen catch 25% of the available coral trout population each year! Fortunately a third of all reefs are now closed to fishing and provide a refuge for these heavily targeted fishes.

A substantial inshore commercial net fishery operates in the World Heritage Area, with another 300 vessels taking a further 2800 tonnes of fish from waters near the coast. On top of that, small fisheries exist in the Great Barrier Reef World Heritage Area for rock lobsters, bêche-de-mer, corals and trochus shells, as well as the operations of 50 licensed aquarium fish collectors. The redundancy built into the complex feeding network of the reef community ensures that the overall impact of removing these target species from the ecosystem is minimal.

The Great Barrier Reef is also used as a highway by coastal and international shipping, with about 6000 vessels over 50 metres long passing through reef waters each year. Over 50% of these boats are bulk carriers, shipping coal, bauxite, sugar, silica sand or alumina to overseas markets; another 25% are large container ships. Many of the large coal ships have a total loaded weight of over 100,000 tonnes. The main shipping channel traverses the entire length of the World Heritage Area between the outer reefs and the coast, with another three passages running from the inner channel out through the reefs to the open sea. An alternative outer channel runs through the Coral Sea, from Torres Strait down the outside of the reef to Sandy Cape, but is a more exposed and treacherous route. Pilotage is compulsory through the narrow, winding coastal channel north of Cairns where an average of seven large vessels pass through the shipping channel each day. Given this high volume of large ships operating in close proximity to coral reefs, it is not surprising that an average of one to two groundings occur every year. So far there have been no oil spills resulting from these groundings and all vessels have been successfully refloated.

Unquestionably, the most important human activity on the Great Barrier Reef is tourism, with a total of around two million people visiting the reef every year. The economic benefit to Australia is estimated at a billion dollars annually. Most tourists take advantage of daytrips on large vessels that operate out of Cairns and Port Douglas, where the offshore reefs are only 30–50 kilometres from the coast. Smaller centres of activity exist offshore from the Whitsunday Islands and in the Capricorn–Bunker Group of reefs offshore from Gladstone. Large operations often use a destination pontoon permanently moored on the protected side of an offshore reef, which acts as a base for visitors as they explore the reef. Glass-bottomed boats and semi-submersibles enhance the reef experience and guided snorkelling and diving activities allow visitors to get up-close-and-personal with reef inhabitants. The high-speed catamarans that make daily runs to these pontoons can carry 200–400 people in comfort. Smaller boats ferry more-intimate diving and snorkelling groups and a number of live-aboard vessels cater for extended dive trips to more remote parts of the reef.

Researchers also have a presence on the Great Barrier Reef, with four offshore research stations situated on islands and cays and a number of large research boats making regular expeditions to all parts of the reef. Despite 30 years of intense research effort, scientists have only really dipped their toes into the unfathomable mystery of this magnificent ecosystem.

Opposite: A snorkeller wonders at a field of vase coral *Turbinaria mesenterina*.

Diving is one of the Great Barrier Reef's biggest drawcards and many reefs are now accessible to scuba divers. While some corals are fragile, and careless divers occasionally break some of their branches, this does not harm the corals and broken fragments often initiate the growth of new colonies. Even in heavily used pontoon sites very little coral mortality results from reef visitors.

A diver examines a staghorn *Acropora* coral.

Resorts are located on a number of offshore islands and cays on the Great Barrier Reef, accommodating those visitors who wish to stay and experience the reef in all its many moods. At low tide, it is possible to explore the reef flat around these cays and islands. Cautious walking on sand and dead coral "pavement" limits damage to the reef during these excursions.

Exploring a shallow reef flat on foot is an enlightening and educative experience for visitors to the World Heritage Area.

DISCOVERY

The vast continent of Australia has been thoroughly explored. Seismic shot lines have been run across the remotest deserts, geologists and biologists have combed the country and all that remains for modern day explorers is the somewhat lesser thrill of personal discovery.

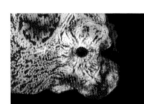

Australia's botany is now well documented, and it has been many years since the scientific community experienced the thrill of unearthing a new terrestrial mammal species, but the joys of discovery are still highly possible once we enter the Great Barrier Reef's coral realm. A new dolphin species was named as recently as 2005, and new fishes are regularly discovered. Many unknown species still await discovery, especially in the dark blue world of the deep reef below 50 metres. It is not just scientists who uncover new reef animals — many new species identified over the past 20 years have been discovered by interested amateurs. The tremendous thrill and sense of achievement that comes from making a new discovery on the Great Barrier Reef is something that is becoming increasingly unattainable in our cloistered existence on terra firma.

Of course, the feeling that comes from breaking new ground is not only the result of discovering new species. Wherever we tread in Australia we are sure to be following in many people's footsteps, but once we begin to delve into the Great Barrier Reef we find there are many places unspoilt by the touch of human hands. Even in the 21st century, the underwater world of many reefs remains unexplored and there are still many exciting new dive sites awaiting inspection, areas just as pristine (and more life-sustaining) than the surface of our most distant planets. Every dive made with an awareness of the Great Barrier Reef's astonishing diversity brings with it new insights and fresh perspectives that may ultimately lead to important breakthroughs in our overall comprehension of the reef. Once again, it is not only marine scientists who bring us these new ideas and discoveries — any enthusiastic diver can contribute to our knowledge of this majestic ecosystem.

More important, however, than any of these physical discoveries are the personal (some might say spiritual) discoveries awaiting visitors to the vast Great Barrier Reef World Heritage Area. The trappings of the modern world are swiftly shed once a diver or snorkeller enters the water. Beneath the waves all is peaceful, conversation is impossible and the vibrancy and diversity of the reef community banishes from our minds the petty neuroses of everyday life. Unlike much of our terrestrial world, the reef remains unbridled — a truly wild environment that has suffered little modification by humans. Exploring the Great Barrier Reef often leads to personal growth — growth that stems from conquering a fear of the unknown, which most of us harbour. Often this feeling can transcend our more mundane concerns for sharks, sea snakes or stonefish. Entering the alien world of the reef forces us to face something totally different — to break down and reconcile any preconceived judgements of "otherness".

The bizarre but beautiful head of the male ribbon eel *Rhinomuraena quaesita*.

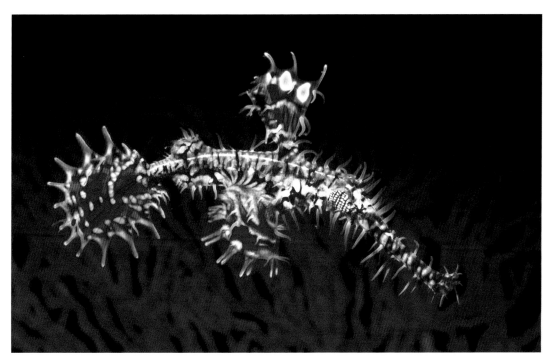

Divers have made many exciting discoveries on the Great Barrier Reef over the past 30 years. As more and more of this huge region undergoes exploration, strange and bizarre species are continually being revealed, proving the ocean is truly Earth's last frontier. Even in the 21st century new species of fishes, animals and plants are still coming to light and many more await discovery.

Tiny pygmy seahorses have recently been discovered by divers around reefs in many parts of the Pacific. Less than 20 millimetres long when they are fully grown, these amazing camouflaged seahorses are almost invisible against the gorgonian fans on which they live. They have been found in Indonesia and diving photographers eagerly anticipate their discovery on the northern Great Barrier Reef.

Pygmy seahorse *Hippocampus bargibanti.*

The longnose hawkfish is quite common in its deep water habitat, but because of its secretive ways and perfect camouflage it is rarely seen by divers. These small, 13-centimetre-long fish nestle on gorgonian fans on steep drop-offs at 30–100 metres depth. To discover these beautiful fish, divers must deliberately seek them out, carefully examining gorgonians on deep reef slopes.

Longnose hawkfish *Oxycirrhites typus.*

THREATS TO THE REEF WILDERNESS

The Great Barrier Reef has developed in an environment that is far from stable. It has endured despite fluctuating sea levels and 6000 years of extreme weather. Over the past 200 years, the pressures of an increasingly disruptive technological civilisation have caused additional stress.

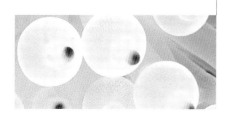

In spite of its World Heritage status, about 24,000 tonnes of seafood is taken from the Great Barrier Reef each year. Fortunately, the fishing industry only targets about ten species of reef fish and only four of these are subject to heavy fishing pressure. Destructive prawn trawling practices have dramatically modified sandy bottom habitats in the Great Barrier Reef lagoon and inter-reef areas. Studies have shown that intensive prawn trawling can remove 70–90% of marine life and completely change the nature of the sandy bottom community. New restrictions on trawling, along with the use of satellite Vessel Monitoring Systems, mean that some of these devastated habitats will eventually recover.

Rapid growth of the tourism market over the past decade has roused concern that we may be loving the reef to death. Will the continuing impact of two million visitors each year disrupt the reef community? Many studies on the effect of intensive, pontoon-based tourist operations (transporting up to 100,000 visitors a year to a single reef site) have shown that tourist use is largely non-damaging and sustainable. Careless snorkellers may break bits off a few coral colonies, but mortality is limited — the overall impact is less destructive than a gale of wind.

There is increasing concern that fertiliser and nutrient run-off from farms has changed the nutrient load of reef waters and may be changing reef communities. Some scientists believe that the destructive plagues of crown-of-thorns sea stars over the past 40 years can be attributed to improved larval survivorship of the sea stars, due to human-generated nutrient increases. A recent scientific review of this problem decided that, while caution was needed, there was no evidence of resultant changes in the World Heritage Area ecosystem from farm and commercial run-off.

Global warming is perhaps the greatest threat to the reef. Scientists anticipate that warming sea temperatures will cause a corresponding increase in the frequency and severity of cyclones; however, the damage caused to reefs by more frequent cyclones would be minimal compared to the impact that may be caused by warmer waters themselves. Coral bleaching results from sustained high summer sea temperatures and it is anticipated that global warming will increase the severity and frequency of bleaching episodes. Large inshore areas of the Arabian Gulf are already coral wastelands from repeated bleaching events over the past decade, and the Great Barrier Reef has suffered two destructive bleaching events over the same period.

In this ever-crowded world it is becoming increasingly difficult to escape the proximity of our fellow humans. People are aware of the importance of regular respite from the constant pressure of social interactions and many realise the experience offered by remote, unpopulated regions gives them the break they need to keep a sense of perspective in their busy lives. Increasing populations make it harder and harder to find these precious wilderness experiences on land. Even on remote tracks in the middle of the Simpson Desert a constant stream of 4WD vehicles can spoil our sense of solitude. However, once the 30 frequently visited reefs of the Great Barrier Reef are left behind wilderness is a fact of life. Apart from the odd fishing boat or trawler it is possible to go for days without seeing another soul.

South of the Whitsunday Islands the outer reefs tend further offshore beyond the reach of even the fastest day boats. In the Pompey and Swain Groups there are almost 1000 offshore reefs that are only visited by fishermen and a few live-aboard charter boats. All these reefs are completely beyond the sight of land and the feeling of wilderness and isolation experienced during a visit to this area is profound. The northern offshore reefs provide a similar feeling of isolation, especially in the large area of protected green zone offshore from Shelburne Bay.

Diving itself provides a similar experience of wilderness and isolation. The alien world we immerse ourselves within compels us to live in the moment. The amazing experience of being surrounded by teeming coral reef animals and fishes enforces a sustained appreciation for the immediate instant. Once we are underwater the limited visibility blocks out boats and other people and the lack of communication means that we feel alone even when swimming close to our buddy diver. A day of diving in the great wilderness of the Great Barrier Reef World Heritage Area instills a sense of relaxation and renewal that lets us return to the real world with newfound enthusiasm.

Opposite: Allied cowrie *Crenavolva rosewateri* feeding on a gorgonian. Despite the reef's perceived fragility to our collective human touch, it is global warming, not increased tourism, that poses the greatest threat.

Lying far beyond the haste of the modern world, the reef imparts a feeling of wilderness and serenity that helps people consolidate their stress and sanity levels. Only a few reefs and islands in this vast area are frequently visited. Once we enter the water and our minds become engaged by the amazing diversity that surrounds us, it is easy to let go of the concerns of everyday existence.

Snorkellers exploring the tranquil reef flat near Heron Island.

A school of purple queens *Pseudanthias tuka* surround a golden damsel *Amblyglyphidodon aureus* in a staghorn *Acropora* thicket. The calming, hypnotic effect of watching fishes is felt by many visitors to the reef.

The 1991 Gulf War provided a vivid demonstration of the impact of a massive oil spill in a tropical marine environment. An estimated 1.5 million tonnes of crude oil was released into the Arabian Gulf, most of it ending up on a shallow region of coral reefs and seagrass meadows along the coast of Saudi Arabia. Scientists were surprised to find that short-term damage was limited and, remarkably, fifteen years later these habitats appeared in better health than ever. Oil is a floating organic material that is rapidly broken down by bacterial action in high-energy marine habitats like coral reefs.

A clump of healthy *Acropora* stony corals.

The biggest threat to the future health of the Great Barrier Reef appears to be global warming. When water temperatures around the reef rise above 31 °C the photosynthesis process of the zooxanthellae in the corals starts to produce deadly toxic by-products. When this happens, the algae are expelled from the corals' tissues. Because these symbiotic algae provide the stony corals' colour, the corals appear bleached white without them. Unless the temperature drops within a few weeks and allows the corals to regain their algae, the corals will die. Damaging bleaching events occurred on the reef in 1998 and 2002 and continued temperature increases could severely compromise the health of the Great Barrier Reef.

Above, left to right: Bleached staghorn branches *Acropora microphthalma*; Spine-cheek anemonefish *Premnas biaculeatus* in an anemone that has been bleached by high water temperatures.

The Great Barrier Reef is a limitless source of beauty and wonder. Fantastic colours and shapes abound, all of them leading us to find out more about the animals and plants that inhabit this unique World Heritage Area.

Above: Daisy corals *Tubastrea* sp. with polyps expanded at night.

Opposite: A trio of roundface batfishes *Platax teira*. This species is naturally curious and often closely scrutinise divers.

ABOUT THE AUTHOR — DR TONY AYLING

Tony Ayling decided to become a marine biologist when he was ten years old and has followed his dreams ever since. He started scuba diving at the age of fourteen and is now a veteran in his field — having spent more than 10,000 hours observing marine life in its natural habitat.

Tony completed his university study in Auckland, New Zealand, where he obtained a doctorate in Marine Biology in 1977. A short time later he married another marine biologist, and moved to north Queensland to live and work on the Great Barrier Reef. Since then Tony has been fortunate enough to explore and study most regions of the reef and has spent over 25 years researching fishes, corals and other reef animals and plants. He is especially interested in fish classification and behaviour and has written a book on the sea fishes of New Zealand.

Dr Tony Ayling lives with his partner, Avril, and twin daughters, Bliss and Xenica, in the Daintree rainforest and still dives regularly all over the Great Barrier Reef. He also enjoys writing and recently contributed his extensive and intimate knowledge of marine life to four titles in the Steve Parish KIDS Fact File range.

DEDICATION

This book is dedicated to Avril who has provided friendship and inspiration for so many years.

AUTHOR'S ACKNOWLEDGEMENTS

This book is a distillation of what I think is important to know about the Great Barrier Reef World Heritage Area after more than 25 years of diving research and survey work all around the reef.

Spending between three and six months in the field every year, on the far flung reaches of the GBR, is quite a logistic exercise and I would like to thank all the capable skippers, deckies and cooks from the many boats I have spent time on over the years, especially Harry Johnson and Robyn Springett, Cocky Watkins, Ron Isbel, and Monty and Daphne Craven. Thanks are also due to the staff of the Lizard Island Research Station, Anne Hoggett, Lyle Vail and Maryanne, Lance Pierce, and former staff Barry and Lois Goldman.

I would also like to thank all my dive buddies who have helped with the diving, often in hard conditions, especially Warren Nott, Gabe Codina, Chris Ryan, Chrissy Maguire, Cathy Bone, Parish Robbins, Nik Taylor, Dave Williamson, Jamie Colquhoun, Ian Douglas and Steve Neale.

Discussions, work and play with my many marine biological colleagues has increased my knowledge of the reef and shaped my understanding of the workings of the coral reef ecosystem. Thanks to you all, including Howard Choat, Geoff Jones, Mark McCormick, Charlie Veron, Terry Done, Peter Doherty, Dave Williams, Uschi Kaly, Mike Kingsford, Rob Van Woesik, Rick Braley, Barry Russell, Emma Gyuris, Chris Battershill and Gary Russ.

The staff of the Research and Monitoring section of the Great Barrier Reef Marine Park Authority provided a lot of help over the years and I thank them all, especially Wendy Craik, Ray Berkelmans and Andrew Chin.

My special thanks must go to Wade and Jan Doak, who provided some of my earliest inspiration.

Finally, I must make a special vote of thanks to my wonderful children Bliss and Xenica for putting up with long absences and proving to me that all things are possible.

Without Avril, my partner and work mate of 30 years, none of this would have been possible — thanks from the bottom of my heart.

ABOUT THE PHOTOGRAPHER — GARY BELL

Gary Bell is a professional wildlife photographer who has been diving and photographing the Great Barrier Reef for more than 30 years.

Since taking his first underwater photograph beneath Portsea pier in 1975, Gary has become recognised as one of the worlds' most accomplished underwater photographers. His photographic assignments have taken him all over Australia and the Pacific, working on consignment for National Geographic Society magazine and TV division, *Australian Geographic* and CSIRO Division of Fisheries. He has also worked on assignment with David Doubilet, assisting Doubilet on more than seventeen *National Geographic* magazine field assignments.

Gary's creative style has won him several international awards, including the Australasia Underwater Photographer of the Year in 1990, 1991, and 1992 — he is the only person to have ever won this award in three consecutive years.

In 2003, Gary launched OceanwideImages.com — one of the world's most comprehensive collections of marine life pictures. It features Gary's own images and images by other award-winning photographers.

When not exploring the undersea world with his camera, Gary is equally at home photographing terrestrial wildlife in the Australian outback. He lives in Coffs Harbour, on the New South Wales' mid north coast, with his wife, Meri, and their two children, Leah and Adam.

DEDICATION

I dedicate this book to my wife,
Meri, daughter Leah and son Adam.

PHOTOGRAPHER'S ACKNOWLEDGEMENTS

Underwater photography usually requires a great deal of help and assistance and without this the images in this book could not have been made. I would especially like to thank the following people for their support over the years.

First and foremost I would like to thank my wonderful wife, Meri, for her undivided support, encouragement and patience. Meri is the driving force behind all of my photographic achievements; she is my companion above and below water and the calm in my life — together we have shared some incredible adventures beneath the sea.

I wish to express my sincere appreciation to my publisher, Steve Parish. Steve is an extraordinarily talented man and without his creative photographic vision, this book may have never come to fruition.

A special thank you must go to Bob Halstead for allowing me to include in the book his spectacular spawning sea cucumber image and blue-ringed octopus image. David Doubilet taught me how to see light underwater and more importantly, how to record light — I value every moment we have shared in the sea. Bill and Peter Boyle have been there since the very beginning and together we learned how to photograph fish underwater. In my early days, Geoff Skinner very generously set me up with an Oceanic Hydro 35 underwater camera housing so that I could take better pictures and arranged my first photographic assignment on the Great Barrier Reef. Libby Grant, Mark McKillop, Wendy Evans, Grant Bailey, Ron and Valerie Taylor, Ron Isbell, Dean Lea, Mike Osmond and Mark Simmons helped and encouraged me greatly during my three years on Heron Island. Karen Gowlett-Holmes taught me how to find the seemingly invisible creatures that live in the sea. Fish Taxonomist and electronics genius, Rudie Kuiter, has kindly identified many of the fish in my pictures and advised me on the technical aspects of underwater photography. John and Bob Evetts generously invited Meri and I to join them on several of their *Elizabeth EII* adventures to remote areas of the Great Barrier Reef and during these excursions I was able to take many pictures that would have not otherwise been taken. Phil Hobbs and the crew of *Tusa IV* plotted our path to the far northern reaches of the Great Barrier Reef and took us on an adventure of a lifetime.

To each and every one of these people, I express my heartfelt thanks and appreciation.

PHOTOGRAPHIC NOTES

My interest in underwater photography began in 1975, when I made my first photograph with a Nikonos camera. I was instantly captivated by my new hobby and lived for photography, but even more so I fell in love with the sea. I still use this camera today, as it takes wonderful underwater pictures.

There is no question that underwater photography is a challenge. However, the difficulties associated with the profession, such as bulky equipment, often-unfavourable conditions and discomfort, are far outweighed by experiences of extraordinary beauty and exquisite moments.

My primary objective these days is to record pieces of time in the sea — special moments, which I share with others, mostly through published materials. To be a successful underwater photographer, I believe one must first have respect for both the sea and its creatures.

The photographs in this book were made with 35mm film cameras over a time period stretching three decades. I used the following equipment:

CAMERAS:

Some of my early underwater photographs were made using Nikon F3 cameras in an Oceanic Hydro 35 housing and Aqua-vision Aquatica III housings. I later switched to using Nikon F4 cameras in Aqua-vision Aquatica IV housings and Nexus F4 and F4 Pro housings. I also used Nikonos III and V cameras with 15mm f2.8 u/w Nikkor lenses.

The above-water photographs were made using Nikon F3, F4 and F100 cameras.

LENSES:

For the underwater wide-angle and seascape photographs, I used a Nikkor 16mm f2.8 full frame fish-eye, 20mm f2.8, 24mm f2.8 and 28mm f2.8 lens. For the fish and invertebrate life photographs, I mostly used a Nikkor 55mm f2.8 micro, 60mm f2.8 micro and 105mm f2.8 micro lens. The extreme close-up photographs were made with a Nikkor 105mm micro lens fitted with a Nikon 4T diopter and Kenko 1.5X converter. My favourite lenses underwater are the 16mm fish-eye and 105mm micro.

For the above-water photographs I used the following Nikkor lenses: 16mm fish-eye, 24mm, 28mm, 105mm micro, 80-200mm f2.8 silent-wave zoom and 300mm f2.8 with a Nikon TC-14E converter.

STROBES:

I used twin Sea & Sea YS-150 and twin Sea & Sea YS-200 manual strobes with Sea-Lock wet connectors for the wide-angle and seascape photographs. For the fish and invertebrate life photographs, I mostly used twin Sea & Sea YS-120 TTL strobes with Nikonos connectors. Some wide-angle photographs were shot with a Nikonos and 15mm lens using a single YS 200 strobe, which I held by hand. I like the Sea-Lock wet flash connectors as they allow me to switch the strobes from camera to camera underwater.

FILM:

Most of the photographs in this book were made with Fujichrome Velvia 50 ISO transparency film. I used Fujichrome Provia 100f ISO film for some wide-angle photographs and a few earlier images were made with Kodachrome 64 ISO.

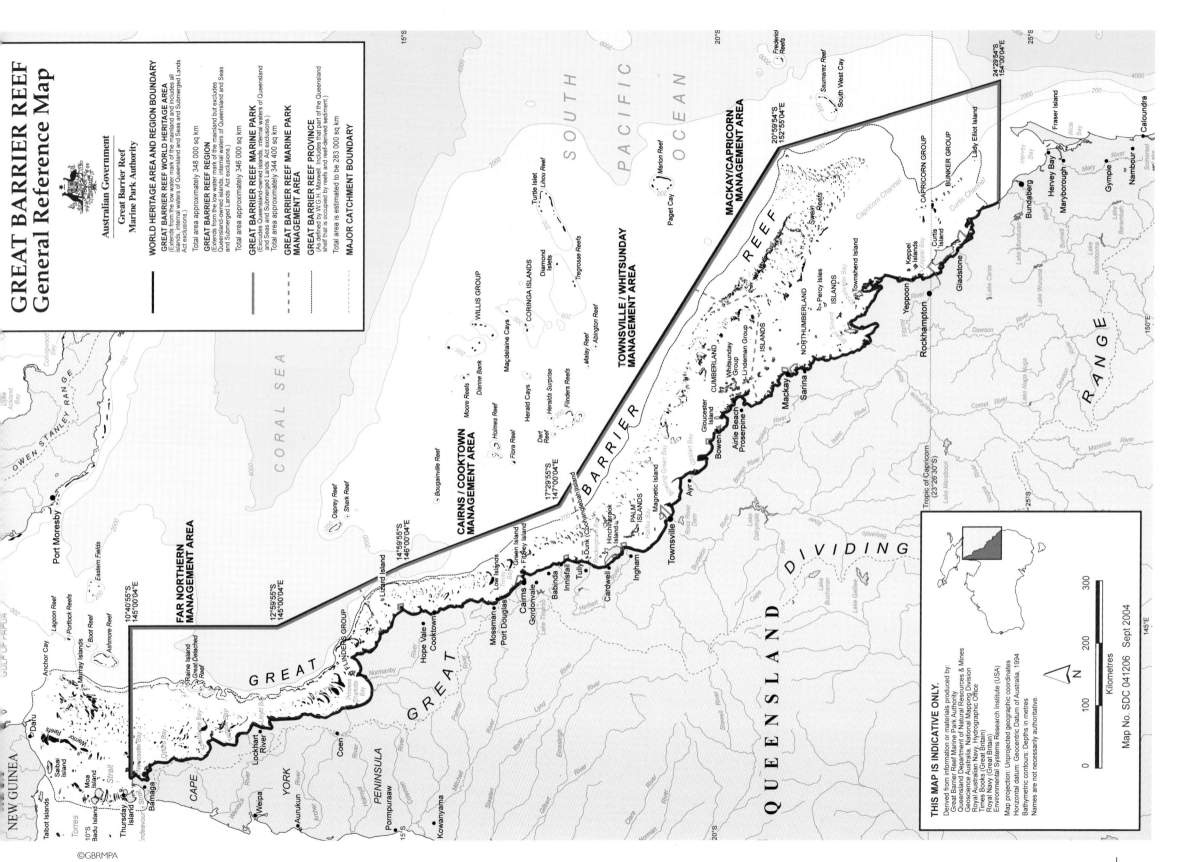

GREAT BARRIER REEF
General Reference Map

Australian Government

**Great Barrier Reef
Marine Park Authority**

WORLD HERITAGE AREA AND REGION BOUNDARY

GREAT BARRIER REEF WORLD HERITAGE AREA
(Extends from the low water mark of the mainland and includes all islands, internal waters of Queensland and Seas and Submerged Lands Act exclusions)

Total area approximately 348 000 sq km

GREAT BARRIER REEF REGION
(Extends from the low water mark of the mainland but excludes Queensland-owned islands, internal waters of Queensland and Seas and Submerged Lands Act exclusions)

Total area approximately 346 000 sq km

GREAT BARRIER REEF MARINE PARK
(Excludes Queensland-owned islands, internal waters of Queensland and Seas and Submerged Lands Act exclusions)
Total area approximately 344 400 sq km

GREAT BARRIER REEF MARINE PARK MANAGEMENT AREA

GREAT BARRIER REEF PROVINCE
(As defined by W.G.H. Maxwell. Includes that part of the Queensland shelf that is occupied by reefs and reef-derived sediment.)

Total area is estimated to be 283 000 sq km

MAJOR CATCHMENT BOUNDARY

THIS MAP IS INDICATIVE ONLY.

Derived from information and materials produced by:
Great Barrier Reef Marine Park Authority
Queensland Department of Natural Resources & Mines
Geoscience Australia, National Mapping Division
Royal Australian Navy, Hydrographic Office
Times Books (Great Britain)
Royal Navy (Great Britain)
Environmental Systems Research Institute (USA)

Map projection: Unprojected geographic coordinates
Horizontal datum: Geocentric Datum of Australia, 1994
Bathymetric contours: Depths in metres
Names are not necessarily authoritative.

Map No. SDC 041206   Sept 2004

©GBRMPA

INDEX

Galeocerdo cuvier 196

A school of male and female orange fairy basslets *Pseudanthias squamipinnis* congregate over *Acropora* coral.

Published by Steve Parish Publishing Pty Ltd
PO Box 1058, Archerfield, Queensland 4108 Australia

© copyright Steve Parish Publishing Pty Ltd
ISBN: 978174193131 0
10 9 8 7 6 5 4 3 2 1

Photography: Gary Bell
Additional photography: Bob Halstead/OceanwideImages.com: pp. 122 (left), 123 (left) 180 & 183

Text: Dr Tony Ayling

Design: Gill Stack, SPP

Editorial: Britt Winter; Ted Lewis & Karin Cox, SPP

Production: Tiffany Johnson, SPP

Map courtesy of the Spatial Data Centre, Great Barrier Reef Marine Park Authority
Prepress by Colour Chiefs Digital Imaging, Brisbane, Australia
Printed in China by PrintPlus Limited

Produced in Australia at the Steve Parish Publishing Studios

online
FOR PRODUCTS
www.steveparish.com.au
FOR LIMITED EDITION PRINTS
www.steveparishexhibits.com.au
FOR PHOTOGRAPHY EZINE
www.photographaustralia.com.au